PENGUIN BOOKS — GREAT FOOD

The Well-Kept Kitchen

GERVASE MARKHAM, born in Nottingham in 1568, was a prolific writer and poet. Like many other young men of his time, Markham took up a military career, but after service in The Netherlands and Ireland he turned to writing as a profession. In 1615 he published a handbook for housewives, which remains an important source of early seventeenth-century domestic life and contains instructions for the 'complete woman', from preparing meals to brewing beer and preventing plague and bad breath. Markham died in 1637 and is buried at St Giles's, Cripplegate, London.

The Well-Kept Kitchen

GERVASE MARKHAM

PENGUIN BOOKS

PENGUIN BOOKS

Published by the Penguin Group
Penguin Books Ltd, 80 Strand, London WC2R 0RL, England
Penguin Group (USA) Inc., 375 Hudson Street, New York, New York 10014, USA
Penguin Group (Canada), 90 Eglinton Avenue East, Suite 700, Toronto, Ontario,
Canada M4P 2Y3 (a division of Pearson Penguin Canada Inc.)
Penguin Ireland, 25 St Stephen's Green, Dublin 2, Ireland
(a division of Penguin Books Ltd)
Penguin Group (Australia), 250 Camberwell Road,
Camberwell, Victoria 3124, Australia
(a division of Pearson Australia Group Pty Ltd)
Penguin Books India Pvt Ltd, 11 Community Centre,
Panchsheel Park, New Delhi – 110 017, India
Penguin Group (NZ), 67 Apollo Drive, Rosedale, Auckland 0632, New Zealand
(a division of Pearson New Zealand Ltd)
Penguin Books (South Africa) (Pty) Ltd, 24 Sturdee Avenue,
Rosebank, Johannesburg 2196, South Africa

Penguin Books Ltd, Registered Offices: 80 Strand, London WC2R 0RL, England

www.penguin.com

The English Housewife first published 1615
This extract published in Penguin Books 2011
This edition published for The Book People Ltd, 2011
Hall Wood Avenue, Haydock, St Helens, WA11 9UL

1

All rights reserved

Set in 10.75/13pt Berkeley Oldstyle Book
Typeset by Jouve (UK), Milton Keynes
Printed in Great Britain by Clays Ltd, St Ives plc

Cover design based on a pattern from a tankard made in Southwark, 1630.
Tin-glazed earthenware. (Photograph copyright © Museum of London/Bridgeman
Art Library.) Picture research by Samantha Johnson. Lettering by Stephen Raw

ISBN 978–0–241–96069–1

www.greenpenguin.co.uk

MIX
Paper from
responsible sources
FSC
www.fsc.org   FSC™ C018179

Penguin Books is committed to a sustainable
future for our business, our readers and our
planet. This book is made from paper certified
by the Forest Stewardship Council.

Contents

The inward virtues of every housewife

Having already in a summary briefness passed through those outward parts of husbandry which belong unto the perfect husbandman, who is the father and master of the family, and whose office and employments are ever for the most part abroad, or removed from the house, as in the field or yard; it is now meet that we descend in as orderly a method as we can to the office of our English housewife, who is the mother and mistress of the family, and hath her most general employments within the house; where from the general example of her virtues, and the most approved skill of her knowledges, those of her family may both learn to serve God, and sustain man in that godly and profitable sort which is required of every true Christian.

A housewife must be religious.

First then to speak of the inward virtues of her mind; she ought, above all things, to be of an upright and sincere religion, and in the same both zealous and constant; giving by her example an incitement and spur unto all her family to pursue the same steps, and to utter forth by the instruction of her life those virtuous fruits of good living, which shall be pleasing both to God and his creatures; I do not mean that herein she should utter forth that violence of spirit which many of our (vainly accounted pure) women do, drawing a contempt upon the ordinary ministry, and thinking nothing lawful but the fantasies of their own inventions, usurping to themselves a power of preaching and interpreting the holy word, to which they ought to be but hearers and believers, or at the most but modest persuaders; this is not the office either of good housewife or good woman. But let our English housewife be a godly, constant, and religious woman, learning from the worthy preacher, and her husband, those good examples which she shall with all careful diligence see exercised amongst her servants.

In which practice of hers, what particular rules are to be observed, I leave her to learn of them who are professed divines, and have purposely written of this argument; only thus much I will say, which each one's experience will teach him to be true, that the more careful the master and mistress are to bring up their servants in the daily exercises of religion toward God, the more faithful they shall find them in all their businesses towards men, and procure God's favour the more plentifully on all the household: and therefore a small time morning and evening bestowed in prayers, and other exercises of religion, will prove no lost time at the week's end.

She must be temperate.

Next unto this sanctity and holiness of life, it is meet that our English housewife be a woman of great modesty and temperance as well inwardly as outwardly: inwardly, as in her behaviour and carriage towards her husband, wherein she shall shun all violence of rage, passion, and humour, coveting less to direct than to be directed, appearing ever unto him pleasant, amiable, and delightful; and though occasion, mishaps, or the misgovernment of his will may induce her to contrary thoughts, yet virtuously to suppress them, and with a mild sufferance rather to call him home from his error, than with the strength of anger to abate the least spark of his evil, calling into her mind that evil and uncomely language is deformed though uttered even to servants, but most monstrous and ugly when it appears before the presence of a husband: outwardly, as in her apparel and diet, both which she shall proportion according to the competency of her husband's estate and calling, making her circle rather strait than large, for it is a rule if we extend to the uttermost we take away increase, if we go a hair breadth beyond we enter into consumption, but if we preserve any part, we build strong forts against the adversities of fortune, provided that such preservation be honest and conscionable; for as lavish prodigality is brutish, so miserable covetousness is hellish.

Of her garments.

Let therefore the housewife's garments be comely, cleanly and strong, made as well to preserve the health as adorn the person, altogether without toyish garnishes, or the gloss of light colours, and as far from the vanity of new and fantastic fashions, as near to the comely imitations of modest matrons.

Of her diet.

Let her diet be wholesome and cleanly, prepared at due hours, and cooked with care and diligence; let it be rather to satisfy nature than our affections, and apter to kill hunger than revive new appetites; let it proceed more from the provision of her own yard, than the furniture of the markets, and let it be rather esteemed for the familiar acquaintance she hath with it, than for the strangeness and rarity it bringeth from other countries.

Her general virtues.

To conclude, our English housewife must be of chaste thought, stout courage, patient, untired, watchful, diligent, witty, pleasant, constant in friendship, full of good neighbourhood, wise in discourse, but not frequent therein, sharp and quick of speech, but not bitter or talkative, secret in her affairs, comfortable in her counsels, and generally skilful in all the worthy knowledges which do belong to her vocation.

The outward and active knowledge of the housewife; including her skill in cookery with flesh, fish, sauces, pastry, banqueting and great feasts

To speak then of the outward and active knowledges which belong to our English housewife, I hold the first and most principal to be a perfect skill and knowledge in cookery, together with all the secrets belonging to the same, because it is a duty really belonging to a woman; and she that is utterly ignorant therein may not by the laws of strict justice challenge the freedom of marriage, because indeed she can then but perform half her vow; for she may love and obey, but she cannot serve and keep him with that true duty which is ever expected.

She must know all herbs.

To proceed then to this knowledge of cookery, you shall understand that the first step thereunto is to have knowledge of all sorts of herbs belonging to the kitchen, whether they be for the pot, for sallats, for sauces, for servings, or for any other seasoning, or adorning; which skill of knowledge of the herbs she must get by her own true labour and experience, and not by my relation, which would be much too tedious; and for the use of them, she shall see it in the composition of dishes and meats hereafter following. She shall also know the time of the year, month, and moon, in which all herbs are to be sown; and when they are in their best flourishing, that, gathering all herbs in their height of goodness, she may have the prime use of the same. And because I will enable, and not burden her memory, I will here give her a short epitome of all that knowledge.

Her skill in the garden.

First then let our English housewife know that she may at all times of the month and moon, generally sow asparagus, coleworts, spinach, lettuce, parsnips, radish, and chives.

In February, in the new of the moon, she may sow spike, garlic, borage, bugloss, chervil, coriander, gourds, cresses, marjoram, *palma Christi*, flower-gentle, white poppy, purslane, radish, rocket, rosemary, sorrel, double marigolds, and thyme. The moon full, she may sow aniseeds musked, violets, bleets, skirrets, white succory, fennel, and parsley. The moon old, sow holy thistle, cole cabbage, white cole, green cole, cucumbers, hartshorn, dyer's grain, cabbage-lettuce, melons, onions, parsnips, lark-heel, burnet, and leeks.

In March, the moon new, sow garlic, borage, bugloss, chervil, coriander, gourds, marjoram, white poppy, purslane, radish, sorrel, double marigolds, thyme, violets. At the full moon, aniseeds, bleets, skirrets, succory, fennel, apples of love, and marvellous apples. At the wane, artichokes, basil, blessed thistle, cole cabbage, white cole, green cole, citrons, cucumbers, hartshorn, samphire, spinach, gillyflowers, hyssop, cabbage-lettuce, melons, muggets, onions, flower-gentle, burnet, leeks and savory. In the month of April, the moon being new, sow marjoram, flower-gentle, thyme, violets; in the full of the moon, apples of love, and marvellous apples; and in the wane, artichokes, holy thistle, cabbage-cole, citrons, hartshorn, samphire, gilly-flowers, [muggets], and parsnips. In May, the moon old, sow blessed thistle. In June, the moon new, sow gourds and radishes. The moon old, sow cucumbers, melons, parsnips. In July, the moon at full, sow white succory, and the moon old, sow cabbage-lettuce. Lastly, in August, the moon at full, sow white succory.

Transplanting of herbs.

Also she must know that herbs growing of seeds may be transplanted at all times, except chervil, orach, spinach, and parsley, which are not good being once transplanted, observing ever to transplant in moist and rainy weather.

Choice of seeds.

Also she must know that the choice of seeds are twofold, of which some grow best being new, as cucumbers and leeks, and some being old, as coriander, parsley, savory, beets, origanum, cresses, spinach and poppy; you must keep [from the] cold: lettuce, artichokes, basil, holy thistle, cabbage, cole, dyer's grains, and melons, fifteen days after they put forth of the earth.

Prosperity of seeds.

Also seeds prosper better being sown in temperate weather than in hot, cold, or dry days.

Gathering of seeds.

Seeds must be gathered in fair weather, at the wane of the moon, and kept, some in boxes of wood, some in bags of leather, and some in vessels of earth, and after to be well cleansed and dried in the sun or shadow; othersome, as onions, chibols, and leeks, must be kept in their husks. Lastly, she must know that it is best to plant in the last quarter of the moon; to gather grafts in the last but one, and to graft two days after the change; and thus much for her knowledge briefly of herbs, and how she shall have them continually for her use in the kitchen.

Of cookery and the parts thereof.

It resteth now that I proceed unto cookery itself, which is the dressing and ordering of meat, in good and whole-some manner; to which, when our housewife shall address herself, she shall well understand, that these qualities must ever accompany it: first, she must be cleanly both in body and garments, she must have a quick eye, a curious nose, a perfect taste, and a ready ear (she must not be butter-fingered, sweet-toothed, nor faint-hearted; for the first will let everything fall, the second will consume what it should increase, and the last will lose time with too much niceness). Now for the substance of the art itself, I will divide it into five parts: the first, sallats and fricassees; the second, boiled meats and broths; the third, roast meats, and carbonadoes; the fourth, baked meats and pies; and the fifth, banqueting and made dishes, with other conceits and secrets.

Of sallats. Simple sallats.

First then to speak of sallats, there be some simple, and some compounded; some only to furnish out the table, and some both for use and adornation: your simple sallats are chibols peeled, washed clean, and half of the green tops cut clean away, so served on a fruit dish; or chives, scallions, radish roots, boiled carrots, skirrets, and turnips, with such like served up simply; also, all young lettuce, cabbage lettuce, purslane, and divers other herbs which may be served simply without any-thing but a little vinegar, sallat oil, and sugar; onions boiled, and stripped from their rind and served up with vinegar, oil and pepper is a good simple sallat; so is samphire, bean cods, asparagus, and cucumbers, served in likewise with oil, vinegar, and pepper, with a world of others, too tedious to nominate.

Of compound sallats.

Your compound sallats are first the young buds and knots of all manner of wholesome herbs at their first springing; as red sage, mints, lettuce, violets, marigolds, spinach, and many other mixed together, and then served up to the table with vinegar, sallat oil and sugar.

Another compound sallat.

To compound an excellent sallat, and which indeed is usual at great feasts, and upon princes' tables: take a good quantity of blanched almonds, and with your shredding knife cut them grossly; then take as many raisins of the sun, clean washed and the stones picked out, as many figs shred like the almonds, as many capers, twice so many olives, and as many currants as of all the rest, clean washed, a good handful of the small tender leaves of red sage and spinach; mix all these well together with good store of sugar, and lay them in the bottom of a great dish; then put unto them vinegar and oil, and scrape more sugar over all; then take oranges and lemons, and, paring away the outward peels, cut them into thin slices, then with those slices cover the sallat all over; which done, take the fine thin leaf of the red cauliflower, and with them cover the oranges and lemons all over; then over those red leaves lay another course of old olives, and the slices of well pickled cucumbers, together with the very inward heart of your cabbage lettuce cut into slices; then adorn the sides of the dish, and the top of the sallat with more slices of lemons and oranges, and so serve it up.

An excellent boiled sallat.

To make an excellent compound boiled sallat: take of spinach well washed two or three handfuls, and put it into fair water, and boil it till it be exceeding soft, and tender as pap; then put it into a colander and drain the water from it; which done, with the backside of your chopping knife chop it, and bruise it as small as may be: then put it into a pipkin with a good lump of sweet butter, and boil it over again; then take a good handful of currants clean washed, and put to it, and stir them well together; then put to as much vinegar as will make it reasonable tart, and then with sugar season it according to the taste of the master of the house, and so serve it upon sippets.

Of preserving of sallats.

Your preserved sallats are of two kinds, either pickled, as are cucumbers, samphire, purslane, broom, and such like, or preserved with vinegar, as violets, primrose, cowslips, gillyflowers of all kinds, broom flowers, and for the most part any wholesome flower whatsoever.

Of pickling sallats.

Now for the pickling of sallats, they are only boiled, and then drained from the water, spread upon a table, and good store of salt thrown over them, then when they are thorough cold, make a pickle with water, salt, and a little vinegar, and with the same pot them up in close earthen pots, and serve them forth as occasion shall serve.

Of preserving sallats.

Now for preserving sallats, you shall take any of the flowers before said after they have been picked clean from their stalks, and the white ends (of them which have any) clean cut away, and washed and dried, and, taking a glass pot like a gallipot, or for want thereof a gallipot itself; and first strew a little sugar in the bottom, then lay a layer of the flowers, then cover that layer over with sugar, then lay another layer of the flowers, and another of sugar; and thus do one above another till the pot be filled, ever and anon pressing them hard down with your hand: this done, you shall take of the best and sharpest vinegar you can get (and if the vinegar be distilled vinegar, the flowers will keep their colours the better) and with it fill up your pot till the vinegar swim aloft, and no more can be received; then stop up the pot close, and set them in a dry temperate place, and use them at pleasure, for they will last all the year.

The making of strange sallats.

Now for the compounding of sallats of these pickled and preserved things, though they may be served up simply of themselves, and are both good and dainty, yet for better curiosity, and the finer adorning of the table, you shall thus use them: first, if you would set forth any red flower that you know or have seen, you shall take your pots of preserved gillyflowers, and suiting the colours answerable to the flower you shall proportion it forth, and lay the shape of the flower in a fruit dish; then with your purslane leaves make the green coffin of the flower, and with the purslane stalks, make the stalk of the flower, and the divisions of the leaves and branches; then with the thin slices of cucumbers make their leaves in true proportions, jagged or otherwise: and thus you may set forth some full blown, some half blown, and some in the bud, which will be pretty and curious. And if you will set forth yellow flowers, take the pots of primroses and cowslips, if blue flowers then the pots of violets, or bugloss flowers; and these sallats are both for show and use, for they are more excellent to taste than to look on.

Sallats for show only.

Now for sallats for show only, and the adorning and setting out of a table with numbers of dishes, they be those which are made of carrot roots of sundry colours well boiled, and cut out into many shapes and proportions,

12

as some into knots, some in the manner of scutcheons and arms, some like birds, and some like wild beasts, according to the art and cunning of the workman; and these for the most part are seasoned with vinegar, oil, and a little pepper. A world of other sallats there are, which time and experience may bring to our housewife's eye, but the composition of them and the serving of them differeth nothing from these already rehearsed.

Of fricassees and **quelquechoses**.

Now to proceed to your fricassees, or *quelquechoses*, which are dishes of many compositions and ingredients, as flesh, fish, eggs, herbs, and many other things, all being prepared and made ready in a frying pan; they are likewise of two sorts, simple, and compound.

Of simple fricassees.

Your simple fricassees are eggs and collops fried, whether the collops be of bacon, ling, beef, or young pork, the frying whereof is so ordinary, that it needeth not any relation, or the frying of any flesh or fish simple of itself with butter or sweet oil.

Best collops and eggs.

To have the best collops and eggs, you shall take the whitest and youngest bacon; and, cutting away the sward, cut the collops into thin slices; lay them in a dish, and put hot water unto them, and so let them stand an hour or two, for that will take away the extreme saltness; then drain away the water clean, and put them into a dry pewter dish, and lay them one by one, and set them before the heat of the fire, so as they may toast, and turn them so as they may toast sufficiently through and through: which done, take your eggs and break them into a dish, and put a spoonful of vinegar unto them, then set on a clean skillet with fair water on the fire, and as soon as the water boileth put in the eggs, and let them take a boil or two, then with a spoon try if they be hard enough, and then take them up, and trim them, and dry them; and then, dishing up the collops, lay the eggs upon them, and so serve them up: and in this sort you may poach eggs when you please, for it is the best way and most wholesome.

Of the compound fricassees.

Now the compound fricassees are those which consist of many things, as tansies, fritters, pancakes, and any *quelquechose* whatsoever, being things of great request and estimation in France, Spain, and Italy, and the most curious nations.

To make the best tansy.

First then for making the best tansy, you shall take a certain number of eggs, according to the bigness of your frying pan, and break them into a dish, abating ever the white of every third egg; then with a spoon you shall cleanse away the little white chicken knots which stick unto the yolks; then with a little cream beat them exceedingly together: then take of green wheat blades, violet leaves, strawberry leaves, spinach, and succory, of each a like quantity, and a few walnut tree buds; chop and beat all these very well, and then strain out the juice, and, mixing it with a little more cream, put it to the eggs, and stir all well together; then put in a few crumbs of bread, fine grated bread, cinnamon, nutmeg and salt, then put some sweet butter into the frying pan, and so soon as it is dissolved or melted, put in the tansy, and fry it brown without burning, and with a dish turn it in the pan as occasion shall serve; then serve it up, having strewed good store of sugar upon it, for to put in sugar before will make it heavy. Some use to put of the herb tansy into it, but the walnut tree buds do give the better taste or relish; and therefore when you please for to use the one, do not use the other.

The best fritters.

To make the best fritters, take a pint of cream and warm it; then take eight eggs, only abate four of the whites, and beat them well in a dish, and so mix them with the cream, then put in a little cloves, mace, nutmeg, and saffron, and stir them well together; then put in two spoonful of the best ale barm, and a little salt, and stir it again; then make it thick according unto your pleasure with wheat flour; which done, set it within the air of the fire, that it may rise and swell; which when it doth, you shall beat it in once or twice, then put into it a penny pot of sack: all this being done, you shall take a pound or two of very sweet seam, and put it into a pan, and set it over the fire, and when it is molten and begins to bubble, you shall take the fritter batter, and, setting it by you, put thick slices of well-pared apples into the batter; and then taking the apples and batter out together with a spoon put it into the boiling seam, and boil your fritters crisp and brown: and when you find the strength of your seam consume or decay, you shall renew it with more seam; and of all sorts of seam that which is made of the beef suet is the best and strongest: when your fritters are made, strew good store of sugar and cinnamon upon them, being fair dished, and so serve them up.

The best pancake.

To make the best pancake, take two or three eggs, and break them into a dish, and beat them well; then add unto them a pretty quantity of fair running water, and beat all well together; then put in cloves, mace, cinnamon, and nutmeg, and season it with salt: which done, make it thick as you think good with fine wheat flour; then fry the cakes as thin as may be with sweet butter, or sweet seam, and make them brown, and so serve them up with sugar strewed upon them. There be some which mix pancakes with new milk or cream, but that makes them tough, cloying, and not crisp, pleasant and savoury as running water.

Veal toasts.

To make the best veal toasts, take the kidney fat, and all of a loin of veal roasted, and shred it as small as is possible; then take a couple of eggs and beat them very well; which done, take spinach, succory, violet leaves, and marigold leaves, and beat them, and strain out the juice, and mix it with the eggs: then put it to your veal, and stir it exceedingly well in a dish; then put to good store of currants clean washed and picked, cloves, mace, cinnamon, nutmeg, sugar, and salt, and mix them all perfectly well together; then take a manchet and cut it into toasts, and toast them well before the fire; then with a spoon lay upon the toasts in a good thickness the veal, prepared as before-said: which done, put into your frying pan good store of sweet butter, and when it is well melted and very hot, put your toasts into the same with the bread side upward, and the flesh side downward; and as soon as you see they are fried brown, lay upon the upperside of the toasts which are bare more of the flesh meat, and then turn them, and fry that side brown also: then take them out of the pan and dish them up, and strew sugar upon them, and so serve them forth. There be some cooks which will do this but upon one side of the toasts, but to do it on both is much better. If you add cream it is not amiss.

To make the best panperdy.

To make the best panperdy, take a dozen eggs, and break them, and beat them very well, then put unto them cloves, mace, cinnamon, nutmeg, and good store of sugar, with as much salt as shall season it: then take a manchet, and cut it into thick slices like toasts; which done, take your frying pan, and put into it good store of sweet butter, and, being melted, lay in your slices of bread, then pour upon them one half of your eggs; then when that is fried, with a dish turn your slices of bread upward, and then pour on them the other half of your eggs, and so turn them till both sides be brown; then dish it up, and serve it with sugar strewed upon it.

To make any *quelquechose*.

To make a *quelquechose*, which is a mixture of many things together; take eggs and break them, and do away the one half of the whites, and after they are beaten put to them a good quantity of sweet cream, currants, cinnamon, cloves, mace, salt, and a little ginger, spinach, endive, and marigold flowers grossly chopped, and beat them all very well together; then take pig's pettitoes sliced, and grossly chopped, and mix them with the eggs, and with your hand stir them exceeding well together; then put sweet butter in your frying pan, and, being melted, put in all the rest, and fry it brown without burning, ever and anon turning it till it be fried enough; then dish it up upon a flat plate, and cover it with sugar, and so serve it forth. Only herein is to be observed, that your pettitoes must be very well boiled before you put them into the fricassee.

And in this manner as you make this *quelquechose*, so you may make any other, whether it be of flesh, small birds, sweet roots, oysters, mussels, cockles, giblets, lemons, oranges, or any fruit, pulse, or other sallat herb whatsoever; of which to speak severally were a labour infinite, because they vary with men's opinions. Only the composition and work is no other than this before prescribed; and who can do these need no further instruction for the rest. And thus much for sallats and fricassees.

Additions to the housewife's cookery. To make fritters.

To make fritters another way, take flour, milk, barm, grated bread, small raisins, cinnamon, sugar, cloves, mace, pepper, saffron, and salt; stir all these together very well with a strong spoon, or small ladle; then let it stand more than a quarter of an hour that it may rise, then beat it in again, and thus let it rise and be beat in twice or thrice at least; then take it and bake them in sweet and strong seam, as hath been before showed; and when they are served up to the table, see you strew upon them good store of sugar, cinnamon, and ginger.

To make the best white puddings.

Take a pint of the best, thickest, and sweetest cream, and boil it, then whilst it is hot, put thereunto a good quantity of fair great oatmeal grits very sweet and clean picked, and formerly steeped in milk twelve hours at least, and let it soak in this cream another night; then put thereto at least eight yolks of eggs, a little pepper, cloves, mace, saffron, currants, dates, sugar, salt, and great store of swine's suet, or for want thereof, great store of beef suet, and then fill it up in the farmes according to the order of good housewifery, and then boil them on a soft and gentle fire, and as they swell, prick them with a great pin, or small awl, to keep them that they burst not: and when you serve them to the table (which must be not till they be a day old), first boil them a little, then take them out and toast them brown before the fire, and so serve them, trimming the edge of the dish either with salt or sugar.

Puddings of a hog's liver.

Take the liver of a fat hog and parboil it, then shred it small, and after, beat it in a mortar very fine; then mix it with the thickest and sweetest cream, and strain it very well through an ordinary strainer; then put thereto six yolks of eggs, and two whites, and the grated crumbs of near hand a penny white loaf, with good store of currants, dates, cloves, mace, sugar, saffron, salt, and the best swine suet, or beef suet, but beef suet is the more wholesome, and less loosening; then after it hath stood a while, fill it into the farmes, and boil them, as before showed; and when you serve them to the table, first boil them a little, then lay them on a gridiron over the coals, and broil them gently, but scorch them not, nor in any wise break their skins, which is to be prevented by oft turning and tossing them on the gridiron, and keeping a slow fire.

To make bread puddings.

Take the yolks and whites of a dozen or fourteen eggs, and, having beat them very well, put to them the fine powder of cloves, mace, nutmegs, sugar, cinnamon, saffron, and salt; then take the quantity of two loaves of white grated bread, dates (very small shred) and great store of currants, with good plenty either of sheep's, hog's, or beef suet beaten and cut small; then when all is mixed and stirred well together, and hath stood a while to settle, then fill it into the farmes as hath been before showed, and in like manner boil them, cook them, and serve them to the table.

Rice puddings.

Take half a pound of rice, and steep it in new milk a whole night, and in the morning drain it, and let the milk drop away; then take a quart of the best, sweetest, and thickest cream, and put the rice into it, and boil it a little; then set it to cool an hour or two, and after put in the yolks of half a dozen eggs, a little pepper, cloves, mace, currants, dates, sugar, and salt; and having mixed them well together, put in great store of beef suet well beaten, and small shred, and so put it into the farmes, and boil them as before showed, and serve them after a day old.

Another of liver.

Take the best hog's liver you can get, and boil it extremely till it be as hard as a stone; then lay it to cool, and, being cold, upon a bread-grater grate it all to powder; then sift it through a fine meal-sieve, and put to it the crumbs of (at least) two penny loaves of white bread, and boil all in the thickest and sweetest cream you have till it be very thick; then let it cool, and put to it the yolks of half a dozen eggs, a little pepper, cloves, mace, currants, dates small shred, cinnamon, ginger, a little nutmeg, good store of sugar, a little saffron, salt, and of beef and swine's suet great plenty, then fill it into the farmes, and boil them as before showed.

Puddings of a calf's mugget.

Take a calf's mugget, clean and sweet dressed, and boil it well; then shred it as small as is possible, then take of strawberry leaves, of endive, spinach, succory, and sorrel, of each a pretty quantity, and chop them as small as is possible, and then mix them with the mugget; then take the yolks of half a dozen eggs, and three whites, and beat them into it also; and if you find it is too stiff, then make it thinner with a little cream warmed on the fire;

then put in a little pepper, cloves, mace, cinnamon, ginger, sugar, currants, dates, and salt, and work all together, with casting in little pieces of sweet butter one after another, till it have received good store of butter; then put it up into the calf's bag, sheep's bag, or hog's bag, and then boil it well, and so serve it up.

A blood pudding.

Take the blood of a hog whilst it is warm, and steep in it a quart, or more, of great oatmeal grits, and at the end of three days with your hands take the grits out of the blood, and drain them clean; then put to those grits more than a quart of the best cream warmed on the fire; then take mother of thyme, parsley, spinach, succory, endive, sorrel, and strawberry leaves, of each a few chopped exceeding small, and mix them with the grits, and also a little fennel seed finely beaten; then add a little pepper, cloves and mace, salt, and great store of suet finely shred, and well beaten; then therewith fill your farmes, and boil them, as hath been before described.

Links.

Take the largest of your chines of pork, and that which is called a list, and first with your knife cut the lean thereof into thin slices, and then shred small those slices, and then spread it over the bottom of a dish or wooden platter; then take the fat of the chine and the list, and cut it in the very self same manner, and spread it upon the lean, and then cut more lean, and spread it on the fat, and thus do one lean upon another till all the pork be shred, observing to begin and end with the lean; then

with your sharp knife scotch it through and through
divers ways, and mix it all well together: then take good
store of sage, and shred it exceeding small, and mix it
with the flesh, then give it a good season of pepper and
salt; then take the farmes made as long as is possible, and
not cut in pieces as for puddings, and first blow them
well to make the meat slip, and then fill them: which
done, with threads divide them into several links as you
please, then hang them up in the corner of some chim-
ney clean kept, where they may take air of the fire, and
let them dry there at least four days before any be eaten;
and when they are served up, let them be either fried or
broiled on the gridiron, or else roasted about a capon.

Of boiled meats ordinary.

It resteth now that we speak of boiled meats and broths,
which, forasmuch as our housewife is intended to be
general, one that can as well feed the poor as the rich, we
will first begin with those ordinary wholesome boiled
meats, which are of use in every goodman's house: therefore to make the best ordinary pottage, you shall take a
rack of mutton cut into pieces, or a leg of mutton cut
into pieces; for this meat and these joints are the best,
although any other joint, or any fresh beef will likewise
make good pottage: and, having washed your meat well,
put it into a clean pot with fair water, and set it on the
fire; then take violet leaves, endive, succory, strawberry
leaves, spinach, langdebeef, marigold flowers, scallions,
and a little parsley, and chop them very small together;
then take half so much oatmeal well beaten as there is
herbs, and mix it with the herbs, and chop all very well

together: then when the pot is ready to boil, scum it very well, and then put in your herbs, and so let it boil with a quick fire, stirring the meat oft in the pot, till the meat be boiled enough, and that the herbs and water are mixed together without any separation, which will be after the consumption of more than a third part: then season them with salt, and serve them up with the meat either with sippets or without.

To make ordinary stewed broth.

To make ordinary stewed broth, you shall take a neck of veal, or a leg, or marrow bones of beef, or a pullet, or mutton, and, after the meat is washed, put it into a pot with fair water, and, being ready to boil, scum it well; then you shall take a couple of manchets; and, paring away the crust, cut it into thick slices and lay them in a dish, and cover them with hot broth out of the pot; when they are steeped, put them and some of the broth into a strainer, and strain it, and then put it into the pot; then take half a pound of prunes, half a pound of raisins, and a quarter of a pound of currants clean picked and washed, with a little whole mace and two or three bruised cloves, and put them into the pot and stir all well together, and so let them boil till the meat be enough; then if you will alter the colour of the broth, put in a little turnsole, or red sanders, and so serve it upon sippets, and the fruit uppermost.

A fine boiled meat.

To make an excellent boiled meat: take four pieces of a rack of mutton, and wash them clean and put them into a pot well scoured with fair water; then take a good quantity of wine and verjuice and put into it; then slice a handful of onions and put them in also, and so let them boil a good while; then take a piece of sweet butter with ginger and salt and put it to also, and then make the broth thick with grated bread, and so serve it up with sippets.

To boil a mallard.

To boil a mallard curiously, take the mallard when it is fair dressed, washed, and trussed, and put it on a spit and roast it till you can get the gravy out of it; then take it from the spit and boil it, then take the best of the broth into a pipkin, and the gravy which you saved, with a piece of sweet butter and currants, vinegar, sugar, pepper, and grated bread: thus boil all these together, and when the mallard is boiled sufficiently, lay it on a dish with sippets, and the broth upon it, and so serve it forth.

To make the best white broth.

To make the best white broth, whether it be with veal, capon, chickens, or any other fowl or fish: first boil the flesh or fish by itself, then take the value of a quart of strong mutton broth, or fat kid broth, and put it into a pipkin by itself, and put into it a bunch of thyme, marjoram, spinach, and endive bound together; then when it seethes put in a pretty quantity of beef marrow, and the marrow of mutton, with some whole mace and a few bruised cloves; then put in a pint of white wine with a few whole slices of ginger; after these have boiled a while together, take blanched almonds, and, having beaten them together in a mortar with some of the broth, strain them and put it in also; then in another pipkin boil currants, prunes, raisins, and whole cinnamon in verjuice and sugar, with a few sliced dates; and boil them till the verjuice be most part consumed, or at least come to a syrup; then drain the fruit from the syrup, and if you see it be high coloured, make it white with sweet cream warmed, and so mix it with your wine broth; then take out the capon or the other flesh or fish, and dish it up dry in a clean dish; then pour the broth upon it, and lay the fruit on the top of the meat, and adorn the side of the dish with very dainty sippets; first [trim it with] oranges, lemons, and sugar, and so serve it forth to the table.

To boil any wild fowl.

To boil any wild fowl, as mallard, teal, widgeon, or such like: first boil the fowl by itself, then take a quart of strong mutton broth, and put it into a pipkin, and boil it; then put into it good store of sliced onions, a bunch of sweet pot herbs, and a lump of sweet butter; after it hath boiled well, season it with verjuice, salt, and sugar, and a little whole pepper; which done, take up your fowl and break it up according to the fashion of carving, and stick a few cloves about it; then put it into the broth with onions, and there let it take a walm or two, and so serve it and the broth forth upon sippets: some use to thicken it with toasts of bread steeped and strained, but that is as please the cook.

An excellent way to boil chickens.

If you will boil chickens, young turkeys, peahens, or any house fowl daintily, you shall, after you have trimmed them, drawn them, trussed them, and washed them, fill their bellies as full of parsley as they can hold; then boil them with salt and water only till they be enough: then take a dish and put into it verjuice, and butter, and salt, and when the butter is melted, take the parsley out of the chickens' bellies, and mince it very small, and put it to the verjuice and butter, and stir it well together; then lay in the chickens, and trim the dish with sippets, and so serve it forth.

A broth for any fresh fish.

If you will make broth for any fresh fish whatsoever, whether it be pike, bream, carp, eel, barbel, or such like: you shall boil water, verjuice, and salt together with a handful of sliced onions; then you shall thicken it with two or three spoonful of ale barm; then put in a good quantity of whole barberries, both branches and other, as also pretty store of currants: then when it is boiled enough, dish up your fish, and pour your broth unto it, laying the fruit and onions uppermost. Some to this broth will put prunes and dates sliced, but it is according to the fancy of the cook, or the will of the householder.

Thus I have from these few precedents showed you the true art and making of all sorts of boiled meats, and broths; and though men may coin strange names, and feign strange art, yet be assured she that can do these, may make any other whatsoever; altering the taste by the alteration of the compounds as she shall see occasion: and when a broth is too sweet, to sharpen it with verjuice; when too tart, to sweeten it with sugar; when

27

flat and wallowish, to quicken it with oranges and lemons; and when too bitter, to make it pleasant with herbs and spices.

Additions to boiled meats.
A mallard smored, or a hare, or old cony.

Take a mallard when it is clean dressed, washed, and trussed, and parboil it in water till it be scummed and purified; then take it up, and put it into a pipkin with the neck downward, and the tail upward, standing as it were upright; then fill the pipkin half full with that water in which the mallard was parboiled, and fill up the other half with white wine; then peel and slice thin a good quantity of onions, and put them in with whole fine herbs, according to the time of the year, as lettuce, strawberry leaves, violet leaves, vine leaves, spinach, endive, succory, and such like, which have no bitter or hard taste, and a pretty quantity of currants and dates sliced; then cover it close, and set it on a gentle fire, and let it stew, and smore till the herbs and onions be soft, and the mallard enough; then take out the mallard, and carve it as it were to go to the table; then to the broth put a good lump of butter, sugar, cinnamon; and if it be in summer, so many gooseberries as will give it a sharp taste, but in the winter as much wine vinegar; then heat it on the fire, and stir all well together; then lay the mallard in a dish with sippets, and pour all this broth upon it; then trim the edges of the dish with sugar, and so serve it up. And in this manner you may also smore the hinder parts of a hare, or a whole old cony, being trussed up close together.

To stew a pike.

After your pike is dressed and opened in the back, and laid flat, as if it were to fry, then lay it in a large dish for the purpose, able to receive it; then put as much white wine to it as will cover it all over; then set it on a chafing-dish and coals to boil very gently, and if any scum arise, take it away; then put to it currants, sugar, cinnamon, barberries, and as many prunes as will serve to garnish the dish; then cover it close with another dish, and let it stew till the fruit be soft, and the pike enough; then put to it a good lump of sweet butter; then with a fine scummer take up the fish and lay it in a clean dish with sippets; then take a couple of yolks of eggs, the film taken away, and beat them well together with a spoonful or two of cream, and as soon as the pike is taken out, put it into the broth; and stir it exceedingly to keep it from curding; then pour the broth upon the pike, and trim the sides of the dish with sugar, prunes, and barberries, slices of oranges or lemons, and so serve it up. And thus may you also stew rochets, gurnets, or almost any sea fish, or fresh fish.

To stew a lamb's head and purtenance.

Take a lamb's head and purtenance clean washed and picked and put it into a pipkin with fair water, and let it boil, and scum it clean; then put in currants and a few sliced dates, and a bunch of the best farcing herbs tied up together, and so let it boil well till the meat be enough: then take up the lamb's head and purtenance, and put it into a clean dish with sippets; then put in a good lump of butter, and beat the yolks of two eggs with a little cream, and put it to the broth with sugar, cinnamon, and a spoonful or two of verjuice, and whole mace, and as many prunes as will garnish the dish, which should be put in when it is but half boiled, and so pour it upon the lamb's head and purtenance, and adorn the sides of the dish with sugar, prunes, barberries, oranges, and lemons, and in no case forget not to season well with salt, and so serve it up.

A breast of mutton stewed.

Take a very good breast of mutton chopped into sundry large pieces, and when it is clean washed, put it into a pipkin with fair water, and set it on the fire to boil; then scum it very well, then put in of the finest parsnips cut into large pieces as long as one's hand, and clean washed and scraped; then good store of the best onions, and all manner of sweet pleasant pot herbs and lettuce, all grossly chopped, and good store of pepper and salt, and then cover it, and let it stew till the mutton be enough; then take up the mutton, and lay it in a clean dish with sippets, and to the broth put a little wine vinegar, and so pour it on the mutton with the parsnips whole, and adorn the sides of the dish with sugar, and so serve it up: and as you do with the breast, so may you do with any other joint of mutton.

To stew a neat's foot.

Take a neat's foot that is very well boiled (for the tenderer it is, the better it is) and cleave it in two, and with a clean cloth dry it well from the souse-drink; then lay it in a deep earthen platter, and cover it with verjuice; then

set it on a chafing-dish and coals, and put to it a few currants, and as many prunes as will garnish the dish; then
cover it, and let it boil well, many times stirring it up
with your knife, for fear it stick to the bottom of the
dish; then when it is sufficiently stewed, which will
appear by the tenderness of the meat and softness of the
fruit, then put in a good lump of butter, great store of
sugar and cinnamon, and let it boil a little after; then put
it altogether into a clean dish with sippets, and adorn
the sides of the dish with sugar and prunes, and so serve
it up. And thus for broths and boiled meats.

Of roast meats. Observations in roast meats.

To proceed then to roast meats, it is to be understood
that in the general knowledge thereof are to be observed
these few rules. First, the cleanly keeping and scouring
of the spits and cob-irons; next, the neat picking and
washing of meat before it is spitted,

Spitting of roast meats.

then the spitting and broaching of meat, which must be
done so strongly and firmly that the meat may by no
means either shrink from the spit, or else turn about the
spit: and yet ever to observe that the spit do not go
through any principal part of the meat, but such as is of
least account and estimation: and if it be birds or fowl
which you spit, then to let the spit go through the hollow of the body of the fowl, and so fasten it with picks
or skewers under the wings, about the thighs of the fowl,
and at the feet or rump, according to your manner of
trussing and dressing them.

Temperature of fire.

Then to know the temperatures of fires for every meat, and which must have a slow fire, yet a good one, taking leisure in roasting, as chines of beef, swans, turkeys, peacocks, bustards, and generally any great large fowl, or any other joints of mutton, veal, pork, kid, lamb, or such like, whether it be venison, red or fallow, which indeed would lie long at the fire, and soak well in the roasting; and which would have a quick and sharp fire without scorching, as pigs, pullets, pheasants, partridge, quail, and all sorts of middle sized or lesser fowl, and all small birds, or compound roast meats, as olives of veal, haslets, a pound of butter roasted, or puddings simple of themselves; and many other such like, which indeed would be suddenly and quickly despatched, because it is intended in cookery that one of these dishes must be made ready whilst the other is in eating.

The complexions of meat.

Then to know the complexions of meats, as which must be pale and white roasted (yet thoroughly roasted), as mutton, veal, lamb, kid, capon, pullet, pheasant, partridge, quail, and all sorts of middle and small land or water fowl, and all small birds; and which must be brown roasted, as beef, venison, pork, swan, geese, pigs, crane, bustards, and any large fowl, or other thing whose flesh is black.

The best bastings for meats.

Then to know the best bastings for meat, which is sweet butter, sweet oil, barrelled butter, or fine rendered up seam, with cinnamon, cloves, and mace. There be some that will baste only with water, and salt, and nothing else; yet it is but opinion, and that must be the world's master always.

The best dredging.

Then the best dredging, which is either fine white bread crumbs well grated, or else a little very fine white meal, and the crumbs very well mixed together.

To know when meat is enough.

Lastly to know when meat is roasted enough; for as too much rareness is unwholesome, so too much dryness is not nourishing. Therefore to know when it is in the perfect height, and is neither too moist nor too dry, you shall observe these signs first in your large joints of meat; when the steam or smoke of the meat ascendeth, either upright or else goeth from the fire, when it beginneth a little to shrink from the spit, or when the gravy which droppeth from it is clear without bloodiness, then is the meat enough. If it be a pig, when the eyes are fallen out, and the body leaveth piping; for the first is when it is half roasted, and would be singed to make the coat rise and crackle, and the latter when it is fully enough and would be drawn: or if it be any kind of fowl you roast, when the thighs are tender, or the hinder parts of the pinions, at the setting on of the wings, are without blood, then be sure that your meat is fully enough roasted: yet for a better and more certain assuredness, you may thrust your knife into the thickest parts of the meat, and draw it out again, and if it bring out white gravy without any bloodiness, then assuredly it is enough, and may be drawn with all speed convenient, after it hath been well basted with butter not formerly melted, then dredged as aforesaid, then basted over the dredging, and so suffered to take two or three turns, to make crisp the dredging, then dish it in a fair dish with salt sprinkled over it, and so serve it forth. Thus you see the general form of roasting all kind of meat: therefore now I will return to some particular dishes, together with their several sauces.

Roasting mutton with oysters.

If you will roast mutton with oysters; take a shoulder, a loin, or a leg, and after it is washed parboil it a little; then take the greatest oysters, and, having opened them into a dish, drain the gravy clean from them twice or thrice, then parboil them a little: then take spinach, endive, succory, strawberry leaves, violet leaves, and a little parsley, with some scallions; chop these very small together: then take your oysters very dry drained, and mix them with an half part of these herbs; then take your meat and with these oysters and herbs farce or stop it, leaving no place empty, then spit it and roast it; and whilst it is in roasting take good store of verjuice and butter, and a little salt, and set it in a dish on a chafing-dish and coals; and when it begins to boil, put in the remainder of your herbs without oysters, and a good quantity of currants, with cinnamon, and the yolk of a couple of eggs: and after they are well boiled and stirred together, season it up according to taste with sugar; then put in a few lemon slices, and the meat being enough, draw it and lay it upon this sauce removed into a clean dish, the edges thereof being trimmed about with sugar, and so serve it forth.

To roast a leg of mutton otherwise.

To roast a leg of mutton after an outlandish fashion, you shall take it after it is washed, and cut out all the flesh from the bone, leaving only the outmost skin entirely whole and fast to the bone; then take thick cream and the yolk of eggs and beat them exceedingly well together; then put to cinnamon, mace, and a little nutmeg, with salt, then take bread crumbs finely grated and searced, with good store of currants, and, as you mix them with the cream, put in sugar, and so make it into a good stiffness. Now if you would have it look green, put in the juice of sweet herbs, as spinach, violet leaves, endive, etc. If you would have it yellow, then put in a little saffron strained, and with this fill up the skin of your leg of mutton in the same shape and form that it was before, and stick the outside of the skin thick with cloves, and so roast it thoroughly and baste it very well, then after it is dredged serve it up as a leg of mutton with this pudding, for indeed it is no other: you may stop any other joint of meat, as breast or loin, or the belly of any fowl boiled or roast, or rabbit, or any meat else which hath skin or emptiness. If into this pudding also you beat the inward pith of an ox's back, it is both good in taste, and excellent sovereign for any disease, ache or flux in the veins whatsoever.

To roast a gigot of mutton.

To roast a gigot of mutton, which is the leg splatted, and half part of the loin together; you shall, after it is washed, stop it with cloves, so spit it, and lay it to the fire, and tend it well with basting: then you shall take vinegar, butter, and currants, and set them on the fire in a dish or pipkin; then when it boils you shall put in sweet herbs finely chopped, with the yolk of a couple of eggs, and so let them boil together; then the meat being half roasted you shall pare off some part of the leanest and brownest, then shred it very small and put it into the pipkin also; then season it up with sugar, cinnamon, ginger, and salt, and so put it into a clean dish: then draw the gigot of mutton and lay it on the sauce, and throw salt on the top, and so serve it up.

To roast olives of veal.

You shall take a leg of veal and cut the flesh from the bones, and cut it out into thin long slices; then take sweet herbs and the white parts of scallions, and chop them well together with the yolks of eggs, then roll it up within the slices of veal, and so spit them and roast them; then boil verjuice, butter, sugar, cinnamon, currants, and sweet herbs together, and, being seasoned with a little salt, serve the olives up upon that sauce with salt cast over them.

To roast a pig.

To roast a pig curiously, you shall not scald it, but draw it with the hair on, then, having washed it, spit it and lay it to the fire so as it may not scorch, then being a quarter roasted, and the skin blistered from the flesh, with your hand pull away the hair and skin, and leave all the fat and flesh perfectly bare: then with your knife scotch all the flesh down to the bones, then baste it exceedingly with sweet butter and cream, being no more but warm; then dredge it with fine bread crumbs, currants, sugar, and salt mixed together, and thus apply dredging upon basting, and basting upon dredging, till you have covered all the flesh a full inch deep: then the meat being fully roasted, draw it and serve it up whole.

To roast a pound of butter well.

To roast a pound of butter curiously and well, you shall take a pound of sweet butter and beat it stiff with sugar, and the yolks of eggs; then clap it roundwise about a spit, and lay it before a soft fire, and presently dredge it with the dredging before appointed for the pig; then as it warmeth or melteth, so apply it with dredging till the butter be overcomed and no more will melt to fall from it, then roast it brown, and so draw it, and serve it out, the dish being as neatly trimmed with sugar as may be.

To roast a chine of beef, loin of mutton, lark, and capon at one fire, and at one instant.

If you will roast a chine of beef, a loin of mutton, a capon, and a lark, all at one instant and at one fire, and have all ready together and none burnt: you shall first take your chine of beef and parboil it more than half through; then first take your capon, being large and fat, and spit it next the hand of the turner, with the legs from the fire, then spit the chine of beef, then the lark, and lastly the loin of mutton, and place the lark so as it may be covered over with the beef, and the fat part of the loin of mutton, without any part disclosed; then baste your capon, and your loin of mutton, with cold water, and salt, the chine of beef with boiling lard: then when you see the beef is almost fully enough, which you shall hasten by scotching and opening of it, then with a clean cloth you shall wipe the mutton and capon all over, and then baste it with sweet butter till all be enough roasted; then with your knife lay the lark open which by this time will be stewed between the beef and mutton, and, basting it also, dredge all together; draw them and serve them up.

To roast venison.

If you will roast any venison, after you have washed it, and cleansed all the blood from it, you shall stick it with cloves all over on the outside; and if it be lean you shall lard it either with mutton lard, or pork lard, but mutton is the best: then spit it and roast it by a soaking fire, then take vinegar, bread crumbs, and some of the gravy which comes from the venison, and boil them well in a dish; then season it with sugar, cinnamon, ginger, and salt, and serve the venison forth upon the sauce when it is roasted enough.

How to roast fresh sturgeon.

If you will roast a piece of fresh sturgeon, which is a dainty dish, you shall first stop it all over with cloves, then spit it, and let it roast at great leisure, plying it continually with basting, which will take away the hardness:

then when it is enough, you shall draw it, and serve it upon venison sauce with salt only thrown upon it.

Ordering of meats to be roasted.

The roasting of all sorts of meats differeth nothing but in the fires, speed, and leisure as is aforesaid, except these compound dishes, of which I have given you sufficient precedents, and by them you may perform any work whatsoever: but for the ordering, preparing, and trussing your meats for the spit or table, in that there is much difference; for in all joints of meat except a shoulder of mutton, you shall crush and break the bones well; from pigs and rabbits you shall cut off the feet before you spit them, and the heads when you serve them to table, and the pig you shall chine, and divide into two parts; capons, pheasants, chickens, and turkeys you shall roast with the pinions folded up, and the legs extended; hens, stock-doves, and house-doves, you shall roast with the pinions folded up, and the legs cut off by the knees, and thrust into the bodies; quails, partridges, and all sorts of small birds shall have their pinions cut away, and the legs extended; all sorts of waterfowl shall have their pinions cut away, and their legs turned backward; woodcocks, snipes, and stints shall be roasted with their heads and necks on, and their legs thrust into their bodies, and shovellers and bitterns shall have no necks but their heads only.

To roast a cow's udder.

Take a cow's udder, and first boil it well, then stick it thick all over with cloves: then, when it is cold, spit it, and lay it to the fire, and apply it very well with basting of sweet butter, and when it is sufficiently roasted, and brown, then dredge it, and draw it from the fire; take vinegar and butter, and put it on a chafing-dish and coals and boil it with white bread crumbs, till it be thick: then put to it good store of sugar and cinnamon, and, putting it in a clean dish, lay the cow's udder therein, and trim the sides of the dish with sugar, and so serve it up.

To roast a fillet of veal.

Take an excellent good leg of veal, and cut the thick part thereof a handful and more from the knuckle: then take the thick part (which is the fillet) and farce it in every part all over with strawberry leaves, violet leaves, sorrel, spinach, endive, and succory grossly chopped together, and good store of onions: then lay it to the fire and roast it very sufficiently and brown, casting good store of salt upon it, and basting it well with sweet butter: then take of the former herbs much finer chopped than they were for farcing, and put them into a pipkin with vinegar, and clean washed currants, and boil them well together: then when the herbs are sufficiently boiled and soft, take the yolks of four very hard boiled eggs, and shred them very small, and put them into the pipkin also with sugar and cinnamon, and some of the gravy which drops from the veal, and boil it over again, and then put it into a clean dish, and the fillet, being dredged and drawn, lay upon it, and trim the side of the dish with sugar, and so serve it up.

Of sauces, and first for a roast capon or turkey.

To make an excellent sauce for a roast capon, you shall take onions, and, having sliced and peeled them, boil them in fair water with pepper, salt, and a few bread crumbs: then put unto it a spoonful or two of claret wine, the juice of an orange, and three or four slices of a lemon peel; all these shred together, and so pour it upon the capon being broke up.

Sauce for a hen or pullet.

To make sauce for an old hen or pullet, take a good quantity of beer and salt, and mix them well together with a few fine bread crumbs, and boil them on a chafing-dish and coals, then take the yolks of three or four hard eggs, and, being shred small, put it to the beer, and boil it also: then, the hen being almost enough, take three or four spoonful of the gravy which comes from her and put it to also, and boil all together to an indifferent thickness: which done, suffer it to boil no more, but only keep it warm on the fire, and put into it the juice of two or three oranges, and the slices of lemon peels, all shred small, and the slices of oranges also having the upper rind taken away: then, the hen being broken up, take the brawns thereof, and, shredding them small, put it into the sauce also; and, stirring all well together, put it hot into a clean warm dish, and lay the hen (broke up) in the same.

Sauce for chickens.

The sauce for chickens is divers, according to men's tastes: for some will only have butter, verjuice, and a little parsley rolled in their bellies mixed together: others will have butter, verjuice, and sugar boiled together with toasts of bread: and others will have thick sippets with the juice of sorrel and sugar mixed together.

Sauce for a pheasant or partridge.

The best sauce for a pheasant is water, onions sliced, pepper and a little salt mixed together, and but stewed upon the coals, and then poured upon the pheasant or partridge being broken up, and some will put thereto the juice or slices of an orange or lemon, or both: but it is according to taste, and indeed more proper for a pheasant than a partridge.

Sauce for a quail, rail, or big bird.

Sauce for a quail, rail, or any fat big bird, is claret wine and salt mixed together with the gravy of the bird; and a few fine bread crumbs well boiled together, and either a sage leaf or bay leaf crushed among it according to men's tastes.

Sauce for pigeons.

The best sauce for pigeons, stockdoves, or such like, is vinegar and butter melted together, and parsley roasted in their bellies, or vine leaves roasted and mixed well together.

Sauce for a pig.

To make sauce for a pig, some take sage and roast it in the belly of the pig, then, boiling verjuice, butter, and currants together, take and chop the sage small, and, mixing the brains of the pig with it, put all together, and so serve it up.

Sauce for veal.

To make a sauce for a joint of veal, take all kind of sweet pot herbs, and, chopping them very small with the yolks of two or three eggs, boil them in vinegar and butter, with a few bread crumbs and good store of currants; then season it with sugar and cinnamon, and a clove or two crushed, and so pour it upon the veal, with the slices of oranges and lemons about the dish.

Sauce for a turkey.

Take fair water, and set it over the fire, then slice good store of onions and put into it, and also pepper and salt, and good store of the gravy that comes from the turkey, and boil them very well together: then put to it a few fine crumbs of grated bread to thicken it; a very little sugar and some vinegar, and so serve it up with the turkey: or otherwise, take grated white bread and boil it in white wine till it be thick as a galantine, and in the boiling put in good store of sugar and cinnamon, and then with a little turnsole make it of a high murrey colour, and so serve it in saucers with the turkey in the manner of a galantine.

Of carbonadoes.

Charbonadoes, or carbonadoes, which is meat broiled upon the coals (and the invention thereof first brought out of France, as appears by the name) are of divers kinds according to men's pleasures: for there is no meat either boiled or roasted whatsoever, but may afterwards be broiled, if the master thereof be disposed;

What is to be carbonadoed.

Yet the general dishes for the most part which are used to be carbonadoed are a breast of mutton half boiled, a shoulder of mutton half roasted, the legs, wings, and carcasses of capon, turkey, goose, or any other fowl whatsoever, especially land fowl. And lastly, the uppermost thick skin which covereth the ribs of beef, and is called (being broiled) the Inns of Court goose, and is indeed a dish used most for wantonness, sometimes to please appetite: to which may also be added the broiling of pigs' heads, or the brains of any fowl whatsoever after it is roasted and dressed.

The manner of carbonadoes.

Now for the manner of carbonadoing, it is in this sort; you shall first take the meat you must carbonado, and scotch it both above and below, then sprinkle good store of salt upon it, and baste it all over with sweet butter melted, which done, take your broiling iron; I do not mean a gridiron (though it be much used for this purpose) because the smoke of the coals, occasioned by the dropping of the meat, will ascend about it, and make it stink; but a plate iron made with hooks and pricks, on which you may hang the meat, and set it close before the fire, and so the plate heating the meat behind as the fire doth before, it will both the sooner and with more neatness be ready: then having turned it, and basted it till it be very brown, dredge it, and serve it up with vinegar and butter.

Of the toasting of mutton.

Touching the toasting of mutton, venison, or any other joint of meat, which is the most excellentest of all carbonadoes, you shall take the fattest and largest that can possibly be got (for lean meat is loss of labour, and little meat not worth your time), and, having scotched it, and cast salt upon it, you shall set it on a strong fork, with a dripping pan underneath it, before the face of a quick fire, yet so far off, that it may by no means scorch, but toast at leisure; then with that which falls from it, and with no other basting, see that you baste it continually, turning it ever and anon many times, and so oft that it may soak and brown at great leisure, and as oft as you baste it, so oft sprinkle salt upon it, and as you see it toast so scotch it deeper and deeper, especially in the thickest and most fleshy parts where the blood most resteth: and when you see that no more blood droppeth from it, but the gravy is clear and white; then shall you serve it up either with venison sauce, or with vinegar, pepper and sugar, cinnamon, and the juice of an orange mixed together, and warmed with some of the gravy.

To carbonado tongues.

Take any tongue, whether of beef, mutton, calves, red deer or fallow, and, being well boiled, peel them, cleave them, and scotch them many ways; then take three or four eggs broken, some sugar, cinnamon, and nutmeg, and, having beaten it well together, put to it a lemon cut in thin slices, and another clean peeled, and cut into little four-square bits, and then take the tongue and lay it in; and then having melted good store of butter in a frying pan put the tongue and the rest therein, and so fry it brown, and then dish it, and scrape sugar upon it, and serve it up.

How to boil small fish.

To boil small fish, as roaches, daces, gudgeon, or flounders, boil white wine and water together with a bunch of choice herbs, and a little whole mace; when all is boiled well together, put in your fish, and scum it well: then put in the sole of a manchet, a good quantity of sweet butter, and season it with pepper and verjuice, and so serve it in upon sippets, and adorn the sides of the dish with sugar.

To boil a gurnet or rochet.

First, draw your fish, and either split it open in the back, or joint it in the back, and truss it round, then wash it clean, and boil it in water and salt, with a bunch of sweet herbs: then take it up into a large dish, and pour unto it verjuice, nutmeg, butter, and pepper, and, letting it stew a little, thicken it with the yolks of eggs: then, hot, remove it into another dish, and garnish it with slices of oranges and lemons, barberries, prunes, and sugar, and so serve it up.

To bake a carp.

After you have drawn, washed, and scalded a fair large carp, season it with pepper, salt and nutmeg, and then put it into a coffin with good store of sweet butter, and then cast on raisins of the sun, the juice of lemons, and some slices of orange peels; and then, sprinkling on a little vinegar, close it up and bake it.

How to bake a tench.

First, let your tench blood in the tail, then scour it, wash it, and scald it: then, having dried it, take the fine crumbs of bread, sweet cream, the yolks of eggs, currants clean washed, a few sweet herbs chopped small, season it with nutmegs and pepper, and make it into a stiff paste, and put it into the belly of the tench: then season the fish on the outside with pepper, salt, and nutmeg, and so put it into a deep coffin with sweet butter, and so close up the pie and bake it: then when it is enough, draw it, and open it, and put into it a good piece of a preserved orange minced: then take vinegar, nutmeg, butter, sugar, and the yolk of a new laid egg, and boil it on a chafing-dish and coals, always stirring it to keep it from curding; then pour it into the pie, shake it well, and so serve it up.

How to stew a trout.

Take a large trout, fair trimmed, and wash it, and put it into a deep pewter dish, then take half a pint of sweet wine, with a lump of butter, and a little whole mace, parsley, savory and thyme, mince them all small, and put them into the trout's belly, and so let it stew a quarter of an hour: then mince the yolk of an hard egg, and strew it on the trout, and, laying the herbs about it, and scraping on sugar, serve it up.

How to bake eels.

After you have drawn your eels, chop them into small pieces of three or four inches, and season them with pepper, salt, and ginger, and so put them into a coffin with a good lump of butter, great raisins, onions small chopped, and so close it, bake it, and serve it up.

Of the pastry and baked meats.

Next to these already rehearsed, our English housewife must be skilful in pastry, and know how and in what manner to bake all sorts of meat, and what paste is fit for every meat, and how to handle and compound such pastes. As, for example, red deer venison, wild boar, gammons of bacon, swans, elks, porpoise, and such like standing dishes, which must be kept long, would be baked in a moist, thick, tough, coarse, and long lasting crust, and therefore of all other your rye paste is best for that purpose: your turkey, capon, pheasant, partridge, veal, peacocks, lamb, and all sorts of water fowl which are to come to the table more than once (yet not many days) would be baked in a good white crust, somewhat thick; therefore your wheat is fit for them: your chickens, calves' feet, olives, potatoes, quinces, fallow deer, and such like, which are most commonly eaten hot, would be in the finest, shortest and thinnest crust; therefore your fine wheat flour which is a little baked in the oven before it be kneaded is the best for that purpose.

Of the mixture of pastes.

To speak then of the mixture and kneading of pastes, you shall understand that your rye paste would be

kneaded only with hot water and a little butter, or sweet
seam and rye flour very finely sifted, and it would be
made tough and stiff that it may stand well in the rais-
ing, for the coffin thereof must ever be very deep: your
coarse wheat crust would be kneaded with hot water, or
mutton broth and good store of butter, and the paste
made stiff and tough because that coffin must be deep
also; your fine wheat crust must be kneaded with as
much butter as water, and the paste made reasonable lithe
and gentle, into which you must put three or four eggs or
more according to the quantity you blend together, for
they will give it a sufficient stiffening.

Of puff paste.

Now for the making of puff paste of the best kind, you
shall take the finest wheat flour after it hath been a little
baked in a pot in the oven, and blend it well with eggs,
whites and yolks all together; after the paste is well
kneaded, roll out a part thereof as thin as you please, and
then spread cold sweet butter over the same, then upon
the same butter roll another leaf of the paste as before;
and spread it with butter also; and thus roll leaf upon leaf
with butter between till it be as thick as you think good:
and with it either cover any baked meat, or make paste
for venison, Florentine, tart or what dish else you please
and so bake it. There be some that to this paste use sugar,
but it is certain it will hinder the rising thereof; and therefore when your puffed paste is baked, you shall dissolve
sugar into rose-water, and drop it into the paste as much
as it will by any means receive, and then set it a little
while in the oven after and it will be sweet enough.

Of baking red deer, or fallow, or anything to keep cold.

When you bake red deer, you shall first parboil it and take out the bones, then you shall if it be lean lard it, if fat save the charge, then put it into a press to squeeze out the blood; then for a night lay it in a mere sauce made of vinegar, small drink, and salt, and then taking it forth season it well with pepper finely beaten, and salt, well mixed together, and see that you lay good store thereof, both upon and in every open and hollow place of the venison; but by no means cut any slashes to put in the pepper, for it will of itself sink fast enough into the flesh, and be more pleasant in the eating: then having raised the coffin, lay in the bottom a thick course of butter, then lay the flesh thereon and cover it all over with butter, and so bake it as much as if you did bake great brown bread; then when you draw it, melt more butter, with three or four spoonful of vinegar, and twice so much claret wine, and at a vent hole on the top of the lid pour in the same till it can receive no more, and so let it stand and cool; and in this sort you may bake fallow deer, or swan, or whatsoever else you please to keep cold, the mere sauce only being left out which is only proper to red deer.

To bake beef, or mutton for venison.

And if to your mere sauce you add a little turnsole, and therein steep beef, or ram mutton; you may also in the same manner take the first for red deer venison, and the latter for fallow, and a very good judgement shall not be able to say otherwise than that it is of itself perfect venison, both in taste, colour, and the manner of cutting.

To bake a custard or doucet.

To bake an excellent custard or doucet you shall take good store of eggs, and, putting away one quarter of the whites, beat them exceeding well in a basin, and then mix with them the sweetest and thickest cream you can get, for if it be anything thin, the custard will be wheyish; then season it with salt, sugar, cinnamon, cloves, mace, and a little nutmeg; which done raise your coffins of good tough wheat paste, being the second sort before spoke of, and if you please raise it in pretty works, or angular forms, which you may do by fixing the upper part of the crust to the nether with the yolks of eggs: then when the coffins are ready, strew the bottoms a good thickness over with currants and sugar; then set them into the oven, and fill them up with the confection before blended, and so drawing them, adorn all the tops with caraway comfits, and the slices of dates pricked right up, and so serve them up to the table. To prevent the wheyishness of the custard, dissolve into the first confection a little isinglass and all will be firm.

To bake an olive pie.

To make an excellent olive pie take sweet herbs as violet leaves, strawberry leaves, spinach, succory, endive, thyme, and sorrel, and chop them as small as may be, and if there be a scallion or two amongst them it will give the better taste; then take the yolks of hard eggs with currants, cinnamon, cloves, and mace, and chop them amongst the herbs also; then having cut out long olives of a leg of veal, roll up more than three parts of the herbs so mixed within the olives, together with a good deal of sweet butter; then having raised your crust of the finest and best paste, strew in the bottom the remainder of the herbs, with a few great raisins having the stones picked out; then put in the olives and cover them with great raisins and a few prunes; then over all lay good store of butter and so bake them; then being sufficiently baked, take claret wine, sugar, cinnamon, and two or three spoonful of wine vinegar and boil them together, and then drawing the pie, at a vent in the top of the lid put in the same, and then set it into the oven again a little space, and so serve it forth.

To make a marrow bone pie.

To bake the best marrow bone pie, after you have mixed the crusts of the best sort of pastes, and raised the coffin in such manner as you please, you shall first in the bottom thereof lay a course of marrow of beef mixed with currants; then upon it a layer of the souls of artichokes, after they have been boiled, and are divided from the thistle; then cover them over with marrow, currants, and great raisins, the stones picked out; then lay a course of potatoes cut in thick slices, after they have been boiled soft, and are clean peeled; then cover them with marrow, currants, great raisins, sugar, and cinnamon: then lay a layer of candied eryngo roots mixed very thick with the slices of dates: then cover it with marrow, currants, great raisins, sugar, cinnamon, and dates, with a few damask prunes, and so bake it: and after it is baked pour into it as long as it will receive it white wine, rose-water, sugar, cinnamon, and vinegar, mixed together, and candy all the cover with rose-water and sugar only; and so set it into the oven a little, and after serve it forth.

To bake a chicken pie.

To bake a chicken pie; after you have trussed your chickens, broken their legs and breast bones, and raised your crust of the best paste, you shall lay them in the coffin close together with their bodies full of butter. Then lay upon them, and underneath them, currants, great raisins, prunes, cinnamon, sugar, whole mace, and salt: then cover all with great store of butter, and so bake it; after, pour into it the same liquor you did in your marrow bone pie, with the yolks of two or three eggs beaten amongst it, and so serve it forth.

Additions to the pastry. Venison of hares.

To make good, red deer venison of hares, take a hare or two, or three, as you can or please, and pick all the flesh from the bones; then put it into a mortar either of wood or stone, and with a wooden pestle let a strong person beat it exceedingly, and ever as it is beating, let one sprinkle in vinegar and some salt; then when it is sufficiently beaten, take it out of the mortar, and put it into boiling water and parboil it: when it is parboiled, take it and lay it on a table in a round lump, and lay a board over it, and with weights press it as hard as may be: then, the water being pressed out of it, season it well with pepper and salt: then lard it with the fat of bacon so thick as may be: then bake it as you bake other red deer, which is formerly declared.

To bake a hare pie.

Take a hare and pick off all the flesh from the bones, and only reserve the head, then parboil it well: which done, take it out and let it cool; as soon as it is cold, take at least a pound and a half of raisins of the sun, and take out the stones, then mix them with a good quantity of mutton suet, and with a sharp shredding knife shred it as small as you would do for a chewet: then put to it currants and whole raisins, cloves and mace, cinnamon and salt: then, having raised the coffin longwise to the proportion of a hare, first lay in the head, and then the aforesaid meat, and lay the meat in the true portion of a hare, with neck, shoulders, and legs, and then cover the coffin and bake it as other baked meats of that nature.

A gammon of bacon pie.

Take a gammon of bacon and only wash it clean, and then boil it on a soft gentle fire till it be boiled as tender as is possible, ever and anon fleeting it clean, that by all means it may boil white: then take off the sward, and farce it very well with all manner of sweet and pleasant farcing herbs: then strew store of pepper over it, and prick it thick with cloves: then lay it into a coffin made of the same proportion, and lay good store of butter round about it, and upon it, and strew pepper upon the butter, that as it melts, the pepper may fall upon the bacon: then cover it, and make the proportion of a pig's head in paste upon it, and then bake it as you bake red deer, or things of the like nature, only the paste would be of wheat meal.

A herring pie.

Take white pickled herrings of one night's watering, and boil them a little: then peel off the skin, and take only the backs of them, and pick the fish clean from the bones, then take good store of raisins of the sun, and stone them, and put them to the fish: then take a warden or two, and pare it, and slice it in small slices from the core, and put it likewise to the fish: then with a very sharp shredding knife shred all as small and fine as may be: then put to it good store of currants, sugar, cinnamon, sliced dates, and so put it into the coffin with good store of very sweet butter, and so cover it, and leave only a round vent hole on the top of the lid, and so bake it like pies of that nature. When it is sufficiently baked, draw it out, and take claret wine and a little verjuice, sugar, cinnamon, and sweet butter, and boil them together; then put it in at the vent hole, and shake the pie a little, and put it again into the oven for a little space, and so serve it up, the lid being candied over with sugar, and the sides of the dish trimmed with sugar.

A ling pie.

Take a jowl of the best ling that is not much watered, and is well sodden and cold, but whilst it is hot take off the skin, and pare it clean underneath, and pick out the bones clean from the fish: then cut it into gross bits and let it lie: then take the yolks of a dozen eggs boiled exceeding hard, and put them to the fish, and shred all together as small as is possible: then take all manner of the best and finest pot herbs, and chop them wonderful small, and mix them also with the fish; then season it with pepper, cloves, and mace, and so lay it into a coffin with great store of sweet butter, so as it may swim therein, and then cover it, and leave a vent hole open in the top: when it is baked, draw it, and take verjuice, sugar, cinnamon, and butter, and boil them together, and first with a feather anoint all the lid over with that liquor, and then scrape good store of sugar upon it; then pour the rest of the liquor in at the vent hole, and then set it into the oven again for a very little space, and serve it up as pies of the same nature and both these pies of fish before rehearsed are especial Lenten dishes.

A Norfolk fool.

Take a pint of the sweetest and thickest cream that can be gotten, and set it on the fire in a very clean scoured skillet, and put into it sugar, cinnamon, and a nutmeg cut into four quarters, and so boil it well: then take the yolks of four eggs, and take off the films, and beat them well with a little sweet cream: then take the four quarters of the nutmeg out of the cream, then put in the eggs, and stir it exceedingly, till it be thick: then take a fine man-chet, and cut it into thin shives, as much as will cover a dish bottom, and, holding it in your hand, pour half the cream into the dish: then lay your bread over it, then cover the bread with the rest of the cream, and so let it stand till it be cold: then strew it over with caraway com-fits, and prick up some cinnamon comfits, and some sliced dates; or for want thereof, scrape all over it some sugar, and trim the sides of the dish with sugar, and so serve it up.

A trifle.

Take a pint of the best and thickest cream, and set it on the fire in a clean skillet, and put into it sugar, cinnamon, and a nutmeg cut into four quarters, and so boil it well: then put it into the dish you intend to serve it in, and let it stand to cool till it be no more than lukewarm: then put in a spoonful of the best earning, and stir it well about, and so let it stand till it be cold, and then strew sugar upon it, and so serve it up, and this you may serve either in dish, glass, or other plate.

A calves' foot pie.

Take calves' feet well boiled, and pick all the meat from the bones: then being cold shred it as small as you can, then season it with cloves and mace, and put in good store of currants, raisins, and prunes: then put it into the coffin with good store of sweet butter, then break in whole sticks of cinnamon, and a nutmeg sliced into four quarters, and season it before with salt: then close up the coffin, and only leave a vent hole. When it is baked, draw it, and at the vent hole put in the same liquor you did in the ling pie, and trim the lid after the same manner, and so serve it up.

Oyster pie.

Take of the greatest oysters drawn from the shells, and parboil them in verjuice: then put them into a colander, and let all the moisture run from them, till they be as dry as is possible: then raise up the coffin of the pie, and lay them in: then put to them good store of currants and fine powdered sugar, with whole mace, whole cloves, whole cinnamon, and a nutmeg sliced, dates cut, and good store of sweet butter: then cover it, and only leave a vent hole: when it is baked, then draw it, and take white wine, and white wine vinegar, sugar, cinnamon, and sweet butter, and melt it together; then first trim the lid therewith, and candy it with sugar; then pour the rest in at the vent hole, and shake it well, and so set it into the oven again for a little space, and so serve it up, the dish edges trimmed with sugar. Now some use to put to this pie onions sliced and shred, but that is referred to discretion, and to the pleasure of the taste.

A minced pie.

Take a leg of mutton, and cut the best of the flesh from the bone, and parboil it well: then put to it three pound of the best mutton suet, and shred it very small: then spread it abroad, and season it with pepper and salt, cloves and mace: then put in good store of currants, great raisins, and prunes clean washed and picked, a few dates sliced, and some orange peels sliced: then, being all well mixed together, put it into a coffin, or into divers coffins, and so bake them: and when they are served up open the lids, and strew store of sugar on the top of the meat, and upon the lid. And in this sort you may also bake beef or veal; only the beef would not be parboiled, and the veal will ask a double quantity of suet.

A pippin pie.

Take of the fairest and best pippins, and pare them, and make a hole in the top of them; then prick in each hole a clove or two, then put them into the coffin, then break in whole sticks of cinnamon, and slices of orange peels and dates, and on the top of every pippin a little piece of sweet butter: then fill the coffin, and cover the pippins over with sugar; then close up the pie, and bake it, as you bake pies of the like nature, and when it is baked anoint the lid over with store of sweet butter, and then strew sugar upon it a good thickness, and set it into the oven again for a little space, as whilst the meat is in dishing up, and then serve it.

A warden pie, or quince pie.

Take of the fairest and best wardens, and pare them, and take out the hard cores on the top, and cut the sharp ends at the bottom flat; then boil them in white wine and sugar, until the syrup grow thick: then take the wardens from the syrup into a clean dish, and let them cool; then set them into the coffin, and prick cloves in the tops, with whole sticks of cinnamon, and great store of sugar, as for pippins; then cover it, and only reserve a vent hole; so set it in the oven and bake it: when it is baked, draw it forth, and take the first syrup in which the wardens were boiled, and taste it, and if it be not sweet enough, then put in more sugar and some rose-water, and boil it again a little, then pour it in at the vent hole, and shake the pie well; then take sweet butter and rose-water melted, and with it anoint the pie lid all over, and then strew upon it store of sugar, and so set it into the oven again a little space, and then serve it up. And in this manner you may also bake quinces.

To preserve quinces to bake all the year.

Take the best and sweetest wort, and put to it good store of sugar; then pare and core the quinces clean, and put them therein, and boil them till they grow tender: then take out the quinces and let them cool, and let the pickle in which they were boiled stand to cool also; then strain it through a range or sieve, then put the quinces into a sweet earthen pot, then pour the pickle or syrup unto them, so as all the quinces may be quite covered all over; then stop up the pot close, and set it in a dry place, and once in six or seven weeks look unto it; and if you see it shrink, or do begin to hoar or mould, then pour out the pickle or syrup, and, renewing it, boil it over again, and as before put it to the quinces being cold, and thus you may preserve them for the use of baking, or otherwise, all the year.

A pippin tart.

Take pippins of the fairest, and pare them, and then divide them just in the halves, and take out the cores clean: then, having rolled out the coffin flat, and raised up a small verge of an inch or more high, lay in the pippins with the hollow side downward, as close one to another as may be: then lay here and there a clove, and here and there a whole stick of cinnamon, and a little bit of butter; then cover all clean over with sugar, and so cover the coffin, and bake it according to the manner of tarts; and, when it is baked, then draw it out, and, having boiled butter and rose-water together, anoint all the lid over therewith, and then scrape or strew on it good store of sugar, and so set it in the oven again, and after serve it up.

A codling tart.

Take green apples from the tree, and coddle them in scalding water without breaking; then peel the thin skin from them, and so divide them in halves, and cut out the cores, and so lay them into the coffin, and do in everything as you did in the pippin tart; and before you cover it when the sugar is cast in, see you sprinkle upon it good store of rose-water, then close it, and do as before showed.

A cherry tart.

Take the fairest cherries you can get, and pick them clean from leaves and stalks; then spread out your coffin as for your pippin tart, and cover the bottom with sugar; then cover the sugar all over with cherries, then cover those cherries with sugar, some sticks of cinnamon, and here and there a clove; then lay in more cherries, and so more sugar, cinnamon, and cloves till the coffin be filled up: then cover it, and bake it in all points as the codling and pippin tart, and so serve it; and in the same manner you may make tarts of gooseberries, strawberries, raspberries, bilberries, or any other berry whatsoever.

A rice tart.

Take rice that is clean picked, and boil it in sweet cream, till it be very soft; then let it stand and cool, and put into it good store of cinnamon and sugar, and the yolks of a couple of eggs, and some currants; stir and beat all well together: then, having made the coffin in the manner before said for other tarts, put the rice therein, and spread it all over the coffin; then break many little bits of sweet butter upon it all over, and scrape some sugar over it also; then cover the tart, and bake it, and trim it in all points as hath been before showed, and so serve it up.

A Florentine.

Take the kidneys of veal after it hath been well roasted, and is cold; then shred it as fine as is possible: then take all sorts of sweet pot herbs or farcing herbs, which have no bitter or strong taste, and chop them as small as may be, and, putting the veal into a large dish, put the herbs unto it, and good store of clean washed currants, sugar, cinnamon, the yolks of four eggs, a little sweet cream warmed, and the fine grated crumbs of a halfpenny loaf, and salt, and mix all exceeding well together; then take a deep pewter dish, and in it lay your paste very thin rolled out, which paste you must mingle thus: take of the finest wheat flour a quart, and a quarter so much sugar, and a little cinnamon; then break into it a couple of eggs, then take sweet cream and butter melted on the fire, and with it knead the paste, and, as was before said, having spread butter all about the dish's sides, and rolled out the paste thin, lay it into the dish; then put in the veal, and break pieces of sweet butter upon it, and scrape sugar over it; then roll out another paste reasonable thick, and with it cover the dish all over, closing the two pastes with the beaten whites of eggs very fast together: then with your knife cut the lid into divers pretty works according to your fancy: then set it in the oven and bake it with pies and tarts of like nature: when it is baked, draw it, and trim the lid with sugar, as hath been showed in tarts, and so serve it up in your second courses.

A prune tart.

Take of the fairest damask prunes you can get, and put them in a clean pipkin with fair water, sugar, unbruised cinnamon, and a branch or two of rosemary; and, if you have bread to bake, stew them in the oven with your bread, if otherwise, stew them on the fire; when they are stewed, then bruise them all to mash in their syrup, and strain them into a clean dish; then boil it over again with sugar, cinnamon, and rose-water till it be as thick as marmalade; then set it to cool, then make a reasonable tough paste with fine flour, water, and a little butter, and roll it out very thin; then, having patterns of paper cut in divers proportions, as beasts, birds, arms, knots, flowers, and such like, lay the patterns on the paste, and so cut them accordingly; then with your fingers pinch up the edges of the paste, and set the work in good proportion: then prick it well all over for rising, and set it on a clean sheet of large paper, and so set it into the oven, and bake it hard: then draw it, and set it by to cool: and thus you may do by a whole oven full at one time, as your occasion of expense is: then against the time of service comes, take off the confection of prunes before rehearsed, and with your knife, or a spoon fill the coffin according to the thickness of the verge: then strew it over all with caraway comfits, and prick long comfits upright in it, and so, taking the paper from the bottom, serve it on a plate in a dish or charger, according to the bigness of the tart, and at the second course, and this tart carrieth the colour black.

Apple tart.

Take apples and pare them, and slice them thin from the core into a pipkin with white wine, good store of sugar, cinnamon, a few sanders, and rose-water, and boil it till it be thick; then cool it, and strain it, and beat it very well together with a spoon; then put it into the coffin as you did the prune tart, and adorn it also in the same manner; and this tart you may fill thicker or thinner, as you please to raise the edge of the coffin; and it carrieth the colour red.

A spinach tart.

Take good store of spinach, and boil it in a pipkin with white wine till it be very soft as pap; then take it, and strain it well into a pewter dish, not leaving any part unstrained: then put to it rose-water, great store of sugar and cinnamon, and boil it till it be as thick as marma-lade; then let it cool, and after fill your coffin, and adorn it, and serve it in all points as you did your prune tart, and this carrieth the colour green.

A yellow tart.

Take the yolks of eggs, and break away the films, and beat them well with a little cream; then take of the sweet-est and thickest cream that can be got, and set it on the fire in a clean skillet, and put into it sugar, cinnamon, and rose-water, and then boil it well: when it is boiled, and still boiling, stir it well, and as you stir it, put in the eggs, and so boil it till it curdle; then take it from the fire and put it into a strainer, and first let the thin whey run away into a by-dish, then strain the rest very well, and beat it well with a spoon, and so put it into the tart coffin, and adorn it as you did your prune tart, and so serve it: this carrieth the colour yellow.

A white tart.

Take the whites of eggs and beat them with rose-water, and a little sweet cream: then set on the fire good thick sweet cream, and put into it sugar, cinnamon, rose-water, and boil it well, and as it boils stir it exceedingly, and in the stirring put in the whites of eggs; then boil it till it curdle, and after do in all things as you did to the yellow tart, and this carrieth the colour white, and it is a very pure white, and therefore would be adorned with red caraway comfits, and as this, so with blanched almonds like white tarts, and full as pure. Now you may (if you please) put all these several colours, and several stuffs into one tart, as thus: if the tart be in the proportion of a beast, the body may be of one colour, the eyes of another, the teeth of another, and the talons of another; and so of birds, the body of one colour, the eyes another, the legs of another, and every feather in the wings of a several colour according to fancy; and so likewise in arms, the field of one colour, the charge of another, according to the form of the coat-armour; as for the mantles, trails, and devices about arms, they may be set

out with several colours of preserves, conserves, marmalades, and goodinyakes, as you shall find occasion or
invention, and so likewise of knots, one trail of one
colour, and another of another, and so of as many as
you please.

An herb tart.

Take sorrel, spinach, parsley, and boil them in water till
they be very soft as pap; then take them up, and press
the water clean from them, then take good store of yolks
of eggs boiled very hard, and, chopping them with the
herbs exceedingly small, then put in good store of currants, sugar, and cinnamon, and stir all well together;
then put them into a deep tart coffin with good store of
sweet butter, and cover it, and bake it like a pippin tart,
and adorn the lid after the baking in that manner also,
and so serve it up.

To bake a pudding pie.

Take a quart of the best cream, and set [it] on the fire,
and slice a loaf of the lightest white bread into thin slices,
and put into it, and let it stand on the fire till the milk
begin to rise: then take it off, and put it into a basin, and
let it stand till it be cold: then put in the yolks of four
eggs, and two whites, good store of currants, sugar, cinnamon, cloves, mace, and plenty of sheep's suet finely
shred, and a good season of salt; then trim your pot very
well round about with butter, and so put in your pudding, and bake it sufficiently, then when you serve, strew
sugar upon it.

Of banqueting stuff and conceited dishes.

There are a world of other baked meats and pies, but forasmuch as whosoever can do these may do all the rest, because herein is contained all the art of seasonings, I will trouble you with no further repetitions; but proceed to the manner of making of banqueting stuff and conceited dishes, with other pretty and curious secrets, necessary for the understanding of our English housewife: for albeit they are not of general use, yet in their true times they are so needful for adornation that whosoever is ignorant therein is lame, and but the half part of a complete housewife.

To make paste of quinces.

To make paste of quinces: first boil your quinces whole, and when they are soft pare them and cut the quince from the core; then take the finest sugar you can get finely beaten and searced, and put in a little rose-water and boil it together till it be thick; then put in the cut quinces and so boil them together till it be stiff enough to mould, and when it is cold, then roll it and print it. A pound of quinces will take a pound of sugar, or near thereabouts.

To make thin quince cakes.

To make thin quince cakes, take your quince when it is boiled soft as beforesaid, and dry it upon a pewter plate with a soft heat, and be ever stirring of it with a slice till it be hard; then take searced sugar quantity for quantity and strew it into the quince, as you beat it in a wooden or stone mortar; and so roll them thin and print them.

To preserve quinces.

To preserve quinces; first pare your quinces and take out the cores and boil the cores and parings altogether in fair water, and when they begin to be soft, take them out and strain your liquor, and put the weight of your quinces in sugar, and boil the quinces in the syrup till they be tender; then take them up and boil your syrup till it be thick. If you will have your quinces red, cover them in the boiling, and if you will have them white do not cover them.

To make hippocras.

To make hippocras, take a pottle of wine, two ounces of good cinnamon, half an ounce of ginger, nine cloves, and six pepper corns, and a nutmeg, and bruise them and put them into the wine with some rosemary flowers, and so let them steep all night, and then put in sugar a pound at least; and when it is well settled, let it run through a woollen bag made for that purpose: thus if your wine be claret, the hippocras will be red; if white, then of that colour also.

To make jelly.

To make the best jelly, take calves' feet and wash them and scald off the hair as clean as you can get it; then split them and take out the fat and lay them in water, and shift them: then boil them in fair water until it will jelly, which you shall know by now and then cooling a spoonful of the broth; when it will jelly then strain it, and when it is cold then put in a pint of sack and whole cinnamon and ginger sliced, and sugar and a little rose-water, and boil all well together again: then beat the white of an egg and put it into it, and let it have one boil more: then put in a branch of rosemary into the bottom of your jelly bag, and let it run through once or twice, and if you will have it coloured, then put in a little turn-sole. Also if you want calves' feet you may make as good jelly if you take the like quantity of isinglass, and so use no calves' feet at all.

To make gingerbread.

Take claret wine and colour it with turnsole, and put in sugar and set it to the fire; then take wheat bread finely grated and sifted, and liquorice, aniseeds, ginger, and cinnamon beaten very small and searced; and put your bread and your spice all together, and put them into the wine and boil it and stir it till it be thick; then mould it and print it at your pleasure, and let it stand neither too moist nor too warm.

Marmalade of quinces red.

To make red marmalade of quinces, take a pound of quinces and cut them in halves, and take out the cores and pare them; then take a pound of sugar and a quart of fair water and put them all into a pan, and let them boil with a soft fire, and sometimes turn them and keep them covered with a pewter dish, so that the steam or air may come a little out; the longer they are in boiling the better colour they will have; and when they be soft take a knife and cut them cross upon the top, it will make the syrup go through that they may be all of a like colour: then set a little of your syrup to cool, and when it beginneth to be thick then break your quinces, with a slice or a spoon, so small as you can in the pan, and then strew a little fine sugar in your box's bottom, and so put it up.

Marmalade white.

To make white marmalade you must in all points use your quinces as is beforesaid; only you must take but a pint of water to a pound of quinces, and a pound of sugar, and boil them as fast as you can, and cover them not at all.

To make jumbles.

To make the best jumbles, take the whites of three eggs and beat them well, and take off the veil; then take a little milk and a pound of fine wheat flour and sugar together finely sifted, and a few aniseeds well rubbed and dried; and then work all together as stiff as you can work it, and so make them in what forms you please, and bake them in a soft oven upon white papers.

To make biscuit bread.

To make biscuit bread, take a pound of fine flour, and a pound of sugar finely beaten and searced, and mix them together; then take eight eggs and but four yolks and beat them very well together; then strew in your flour and sugar as you are beating of it, by a little at once; it will take very near an hour's beating: then take half an ounce of aniseeds, coriander seeds, and let them be dried and rubbed very clean, and put them in; then rub your biscuit pans with cold sweet butter as thin as you can, and so put it in and bake it in an oven: but if you would have thin cakes, then take fruit dishes and rub them in like sort with butter, and so bake your cakes on them, and when they are almost baked, turn them and thrust them down close with your hand. Some to this biscuit bread will add a little cream, and it is not amiss, but excellent good also.

To make finer jumbles.

To make jumbles more fine and curious than the former, and nearer to the taste of the macaroon; take a pound of sugar, beat it fine; then take as much fine wheat flour and mix them together, then take two whites and one yolk of an egg, half a quarter of a pound of blanched almonds; then beat them very fine all together with half a dish of sweet butter, and a spoonful of rose-water, and so work it with a little cream till it come to a very stiff paste, then roll them forth as you please: and hereto you shall also, if you please, add a few dried aniseeds finely rubbed and strewed into the paste, and also coriander seed.

To make fresh cheese.

To make an excellent fresh cheese, take a pottle of milk as it comes from the cow, and a pint of cream: then take a spoonful of rennet or earning and put it unto it, and let it stand two hours; then stir it up and put it into a fine cloth, and let the whey drain from it: then put it into a bowl and take the yolk of an egg, a spoonful of rose-water, and bray them together with a very little salt, with sugar and nutmegs; and when all these are brayed together and searced, mix it with the curd, and then put it into a cheese vat with a very fine cloth.

How to make coarse gingerbread.

To make coarse gingerbread, take a quart of honey and set it on the coals and refine it: then take a pennyworth of ginger, as much pepper, as much liquorice; and a quarter of a pound of aniseeds, and a pennyworth of sanders: all these must be beaten and searced, and so put into the honey: then put in a quarter of a pint of claret wine or old ale: then take three penny manchets finely grated and strew it amongst the rest, and stir it till it come to a stiff paste, and then make it into cakes and dry them gently.

How to make quince cakes ordinary.

To make ordinary quince cakes, take a good piece of a preserved quince, and beat it in a mortar, and work it up into a very stiff paste with fine searced sugar: then print it and dry them gently.

How to make cinnamon sticks.

To make most artificial cinnamon sticks, take an ounce of cinnamon and pound it, and half a pound of sugar: then take some gum dragon and put it in steep in rose-water, then take thereof to the quantity of a hazel nut, and work it out and print it, and roll it in form of a cinnamon stick.

To make spice cakes.

To make excellent spice cakes, take half a peck of very fine wheat flour; take almost one pound of sweet butter, and some good milk and cream mixed together; set it on the fire, and put in your butter, and a good deal of sugar, and let it melt together: then strain saffron into your milk a good quantity; then take seven or eight spoonfuls of good ale barm, and eight eggs with two yolks and mix them together, then put your milk to it when it is somewhat cold, and into your flour put salt, aniseeds bruised, cloves, and mace, and a good deal of cinnamon: then work all together good and stiff, that you need not work in any flour after; then put in a little rose-water cold, then rub it well in the thing you knead it in, and work it thoroughly: if it be not sweet enough, scrape in a little more sugar, and pull it all in pieces, and hurl in a good quantity of currants, and so work all together again, and bake your cake as you see cause in a gentle warm oven.

To make Banbury cake.

To make a very good Banbury cake, take four pounds of currants, and wash and pick them very clean, and dry them in a cloth: then take three eggs and put away one yolk, and beat them, and strain them with good barm, putting thereto cloves, mace, cinnamon, and nutmegs; then take a pint of cream, and as much morning's milk and set it on the fire till the cold be taken away; then take flour and put in good store of cold butter and sugar, then put in your eggs, barm, and meal and work them all together an hour or more; then save a part of the paste, and the rest break in pieces and work in your currants; which done, mould your cake of what quantity you please; and then with that paste which hath not any currants cover it very thin both underneath and aloft. And so bake it according to the bigness.

To make the best marchpane.

To make the best marchpane, take the best Jordan almonds and blanch them in warm water, then put them into a stone mortar, and with a wooden pestle beat them to pap, then take of the finest refined sugar well searced, and with it, and damask rose-water, beat it to a good stiff paste, allowing almost to every Jordan almond three spoonful of sugar; then when it is brought thus to a paste, lay it upon a fair table, and, strewing searced sugar under it, mould it like leaven; then with a rolling pin roll it forth, and lay it upon wafers washed with rose-water; then pinch it about the sides, and put it into what form you please; then strew searced sugar all over it; which done, wash it over with rose-water and sugar mixed together, for that will make the ice; then adorn it with comfits, gilding, or whatsoever devices you please, and so set it into a hot stove, and there bake it crispy, and so serve it forth. Some use to mix with the paste cinnamon and ginger finely searced, but I refer that to your particular taste.

To make a paste of Genoa, or any other paste.

To make paste of Genoa, you shall take quinces after they have been boiled soft, and beat them in a mortar with refined sugar, cinnamon, and ginger finely searced, and damask rose-water till it come to a stiff paste; and then roll it forth and print it, and so bake it in a stove; and in this sort you may make paste of pears, apples, wardens, plums of all kinds, cherries, barberries, or what other fruit you please.

To make any conserve.

To make conserve of any fruit you please, you shall take the fruit you intend to make conserve of; and if it be stone fruit you shall take out the stones; if other fruit, take away the paring and core, and then boil them in fair running water to a reasonable height; then drain them from thence, and put them into a fresh vessel with claret wine, or white wine, according to the colour of the fruit: and so boil them to a thick pap all to mashing, breaking, and stirring them together; then to every pound of pap put to a pound of sugar, and so stir them all well together, and, being very hot, strain them through fair strainers, and so pot it up.

To make conserve of flowers.

To make conserve of flowers, as roses, violets, gillyflowers, and such like, you shall take the flowers from the stalks, and with a pair of shears cut away the white ends at the roots thereof, and then put them into a stone mortar or wooden brake, and there crush or beat them till they be come to a soft substance; and then to every pound thereof, take a pound of fine refined sugar well searced and beat it all together, till it come to one entire body, and then pot it up, and use it as occasion shall serve.

To make wafers.

To make the best wafers, take the finest wheat flour you can get, and mix it with cream, the yolks of eggs, rose-water, sugar, and cinnamon till it be a little thicker than pancake batter; and then, warming your wafer irons on a charcoal fire, anoint them first with sweet butter, and then lay on your batter and press it, and bake it white or brown at your pleasure.

To make marmalade of oranges.

To make an excellent marmalade of oranges, take the oranges, and with a knife pare off as thin as is possible the uppermost rind of the orange; yet in such sort as by no means you alter the colour of the orange; then steep them in fair water, changing the water twice a day, till you find no bitterness of taste therein; then take them forth, and first boil them in fair running water, and, when they are soft, remove them into rose-water, and boil them therein till they break: then to every pound of the pulp put a pound of refined sugar, and so, having mashed and stirred them all well together, strain it through very fair strainers into boxes, and so use it as you shall see occasion.

To preserve quinces.

Take quinces and wipe them very clean, and then core them, and as you core them, put the cores straight into fair water, and let the cores and the water boil; when the water boileth, put in the quinces unpared, and let them boil till they be tender, and then take them out and pare them, and ever as you pare them, put them straight into

sugar finely beaten: then take the water they were sodden in, and strain it through a fair cloth, and take as
much of the same water as you think will make syrup
enough for the quinces, and put in some of your sugar
and let it boil a while, and then put in your quinces, and
let them boil a while, and turn them, and cast a good
deal of sugar upon them; they must seethe apace, and
ever as you turn them cover them still with sugar, till
you have bestowed all your sugar; and when you think
that your quinces are tender enough, take them forth,
and if your syrup be not stiff enough, you may seethe
it again after the quinces are forth. To every pound of
quinces you must take more than a pound of sugar, for
the more sugar you take, the fairer your quinces will be,
and the better and longer they will be preserved.

Conserve of quinces.

Take two gallons of fair water, and set it on the fire, and
when it is lukewarm, beat the whites of five or six eggs,
and put them into the water, and stir it well, and then let
the water seethe, and when it riseth up all on a curd,
then scum it off. Take quinces and pare them, and quarter them, and cut out the cores: then take as many pound
of your quinces as of your sugar, and put them into your
liquor, and let it boil till your liquor be as high coloured
as French wine, and when they be very tender, then take
a fair new canvas cloth fair washed, and strain your
quinces through it, with some of your liquor (if they will
not go through easily), then if you will make it very
pleasant, take a little musk, and lay it in rose-water, and
put it thereto; then take and seethe it, until it be of such

substance that, when it is cold, it will cut with a knife; and then put it into a fair box, and if you please, lay leaf gold thereon.

To keep quinces all the year.

Take all the parings of your quinces that you make your conserve withal, and three or four other quinces, and cut them in pieces, and boil the same parings, and the other pieces in two or three gallons of water, and so let them boil till all the strength be sodden out of the said quinces and parings, and if any scum arise whilst it boils, take it away: then let the said water run through a strainer into a fair vessel, and set it on the fire again, and take your quinces that you will keep, and wipe them clean, and cut off the uttermost part of the said quinces, and pick out the kernels and cores as clean as you can, and put them into the said liquor, and so let them boil till they be a little soft, and then take them from the fire, and let them stand till they be cold: then take a little barrel, and put into the said barrel the water that your quinces be sodden in; then take up your quinces with a ladle, and put them into your barrel, and stop your barrel close that no air come into them, till you have fit occasion to use them; and be sure to take such quinces as are neither bruised nor rotten.

Fine ginger cakes.

Take of the best sugar, and when it is beaten searce it very fine, and [take] of the best ginger and cinnamon; then take a little gum dragon and lay it in rose-water all night, then pour the water from it, and put the same, with a little white of an egg well beaten, into a brass mortar, the sugar, ginger, cinnamon and all together, and beat them together till you may work it like paste; then take it and drive it forth into cakes, and print them, and lay them before the fire, or in a very warm stove to bake. Or otherwise take sugar and ginger (as is before said), cinnamon and gum dragon excepted, instead whereof take only the whites of eggs, and so do as was before showed you.

To make suckets.

Take curds, the parings of lemons, of oranges or pome-citrons, or indeed any half ripe green fruit, and boil them till they be tender, in sweet wort; then make a syrup in this sort: take three pound of sugar, and the whites of four eggs, and a gallon of water; then swinge and beat the water and the eggs together, and then put in your sugar, and set it on the fire, and let it have an easy fire, and so let it boil six or seven walms, and then strain it through a cloth, and let it seethe again till it fall from the spoon, and then put it into the rinds of fruits.

Coarse gingerbread.

Take a quart of honey clarified, and seethe it till it be brown, and if it be thick put to it a dish of water: then take fine crumbs of white bread grated, and put to it, and stir it well, and when it is almost cold, put to it the powder of ginger, cloves, cinnamon, and a little liquorice and aniseeds; then knead it, and put it into moulds and print it: some use to put to it also a little pepper, but that is according unto taste and pleasure.

To candy any root, fruit, or flower.

Dissolve sugar, or sugar-candy in rose-water, boil it to a height, put in your roots, fruits, or flowers, the syrup being cold, then rest a little; after take them out and boil the syrup the third time to a hardness, putting in more sugar, but not rose-water; put in the roots, etc., the syrup being cold, and let them stand till they candy.

Ordering of banquets.

Thus having showed you how to preserve, conserve, candy, and make pastes of all kinds, in which four heads consists the whole art of banqueting dishes, I will now proceed to the ordering or setting forth of a banquet; wherein you shall observe that marchpanes have the first place, the middle place, and last place; your preserved fruits shall be dished up first, your pastes next, your wet suckets after them, then your dried suckets, then your marmalades and goodinyakes, then your comfits of all kinds; next, your pears, apples, wardens baked, raw or roasted, and your oranges and lemons sliced; and lastly your wafer cakes. Thus you shall order them in the closet; but when they go to the table, you shall first send forth a dish made for show only, as beast, bird, fish, or fowl, according to invention: then your marchpane, then preserved fruit, then a paste, then a wet sucket, then a dry sucket, marmalade, comfits, apples, pears, wardens, oranges, and lemons sliced; and then wafers, and another dish of preserved fruits, and so consequently all the rest before: no two dishes of one kind going or standing together, and this will not only appear delicate to the eye, but invite the appetite with the much variety thereof.

Ordering of great feasts
and proportion of expense.

Now we have drawn our housewife into these several knowledges of cookery, inasmuch as in her is contained all the inward offices of household, we will proceed to declare the manner of serving and setting forth of meat for a great feast, and from it derive meaner, making a due proportion of all things: for what avails it our good housewife to be never so skilful in the parts of cookery, if she want skill to marshal the dishes, and set every one in his due place, giving precedency according to fashion and custom; it is like to a fencer leading a band of men in rout, who knows the use of the weapon, but not how to put men in order. It is then to be understood, that it is the office of the clerk of the kitchen (whose place our housewife must many times supply) to order the meat at the dresser, and deliver it unto the server, who is to deliver it to the gentlemen and yeomen waiters to bear to the table. Now because we allow no officer but our housewife, to whom we only speak in this book, she shall first marshal her sallats, delivering the grand sallat first, which is evermore compound; then green sallats, then boiled sallats, then some smaller compound sallats. Next unto sallats she shall deliver forth all her fricassees, the simple first, as collops, rashers, and such like; then compound fricassees; after them all her boiled meats in their degrees, as simple broths, stewed broth, and the boilings of sundry fowls. Next them all sorts of roast meats, of which the greatest first, as chine of beef or sirloin, the gigot or legs of mutton, goose, swan, veal, pig, capon, and such like. Then baked meats, the hot first, as fallow deer in pasty, chicken, or calf's-foot pie and doucet. Then cold baked meats, pheasant, partridges, turkey, goose, woodcock, and such like. Then lastly, carbonadoes both simple and compound. And being thus marshalled from the dresser, the sewer, upon the placing them on the table, shall not set them down as he received them, but, setting the sallats extravagantly about the table, mix the fricassees about them; then the boiled meats amongst the fricassees, roast meats amongst the boiled, baked meats amongst the roast, and carbonadoes amongst the baked; so that before every trencher may stand a sallat, a fricassee, a boiled meat, a roast meat, a baked meat, and a carbonado, which will both give a most comely beauty to the table, and very great contentment to the guest. So likewise in the second course she shall first prefer the lesser wild fowl; as mallard, teal, snipe, plover, woodcock, and such like: then the lesser land fowl; as chicken, pigeons, partridge, rail, turkey, chickens, young peahens, and such like. Then the greater wild fowl; as bittern, hern, shoveller, crane, bustard, and such like. Then the greater land fowls; as peacocks, pheasant, pewits, gulls, and such like. Then hot baked meats; as marrow-bone pie, quince pie, Florentine, and tarts.

Then cold baked meats, as red deer, hare pie, gammon of bacon pie, wild boar, roe pie, and such like, and these also shall be marshalled at the table as the first course, not one kind all together, but each several sort mixed together, as a lesser wild fowl and a lesser land fowl; a great wild fowl, and a great land fowl; a hot baked meat, and a cold: and for made dishes and *quelquechoses*, which rely on the invention of the cook, they are to be thrust in, into every place that is empty, and so sprinkled over all the table: and this is the best method for the extraordinary great feasts of princes. But in case it be for much more humble means, then less care and fewer dishes may discharge it; yet, before I proceed to that lower rate, you shall understand that in these great feasts of princes, though I have mentioned nothing but flesh, yet is not fish to be exempted; for it is a beauty and an honour unto every feast, and is to be placed amongst all the several services, as thus; as amongst your sallats all sorts of soused fish that lives in the fresh water; amongst your fricassees all manner of fried fish; amongst your boiled meats, all fish in broths; amongst your roast meats, all fish served hot, but dry; amongst the baked meats, all fish baked, and sea fish that is soused, as sturgeon and the like; and amongst your carbonadoes, fish that is broiled. As for your second course, to it belongeth all manner of shell-fish, either in the shell, or without; the hot to go up with the hot meat, and the cold with the cold. And thus shall the feast be royal, and the service worthy.

Now for a more humble feast, or an ordinary proportion which any goodman may keep in his family for the entertainment of his true and worthy friends, it must hold limitation with his provision, and the season of the year; for summer affords what winter wants, and winter is master of that which summer can but with difficulty have: it is good then for him that intends to feast, to set down the full number of his full dishes, that is, dishes of meat that are of substance, and not empty or for show; and of these sixteen is a good proportion for one course unto one mess, as thus for example; first, a shield of brawn with mustard; secondly, a boiled capon; thirdly, a boiled piece of beef; fourthly, a chine of beef roasted; fifthly, a neat's tongue roasted; sixthly, a pig roasted; seventhly, chewets baked; eighthly, a goose roasted; ninthly, a swan roasted; tenthly, a turkey roasted; the eleventh, a haunch of venison roasted; the twelfth, a pasty of venison; the thirteenth, a kid with a pudding in the belly; the fourteenth, an olive pie; the fifteenth, a couple of capons; the sixteenth, a custard or doucets. Now to these full dishes may be added in sallats, fricassees, *quelquechoses*, and devised paste, as many dishes more, which make the full service no less than two and thirty dishes, which is as much as can conveniently stand on one table, and in one mess; and after this manner you may proportion both your second and third course, holding fullness in one half of the dishes, and show in the other, which will be both frugal in the spender, contentment to the guest, and much pleasure and delight to the beholders. And thus much touching the ordering of great feasts and ordinary entertainments.

The distillations of waters and their virtues

When our English housewife is exact in these rules before rehearsed, and that she is able to adorn and beautify her table, with all the virtuous illustrations meet for her knowledge; she shall then sort her mind to the understanding of other housewifely secrets, right profitable and meet for her use, such as the want thereof may trouble her when need, or time requires.

Of distillations. Of the nature of waters.

Therefore first I would have her furnish herself of very good stills, for the distillation of all kinds of waters, which stills would be either of tin, or sweet earth; and in them she shall distil all sorts of waters meet for the health of her household; as sage water, which is good for all rheums and colics, radish water, which is good for the stone, angelica water good for infection, celandine water for sore eyes, vine water for itchings, rose-water, and eye-bright water for dim sights, rosemary water for fistulas, treacle water for mouth cankers, water of cloves for pain in the stomach, saxifrage water for gravel and hard urine, alum water for old ulcers, and a world of others, any of which will last a full year at the least. Then she shall know that the best waters for the smoothing of the skin, and keeping the face delicate and amiable, are those which are distilled from bean flowers, from strawberries, from vine leaves, from goat's milk, from ass's milk, from the whites of eggs, from the flowers of lilies, from dragons, from calves' feet, from bran, or from yolks of eggs, any of which will last a year or better.

> *Additions to distillations. To distil water of*
> *the colour of the herb or flower you desire.*

First distil your water in a stillatory, then put in a glass of great strength, and fill it with those flowers again (whose colour you desire) as full as you can, and stop it and set it in the stillatory again, and let it distil, and you shall have the colour you distil.

To make aqua vitae.

Take of rosemary flowers two handfuls, of marjoram, winter savory, rosemary, rue, unset thyme, germander, ribwort, hart's tongue, mouse-ear, white wormwood, bugloss, red sage, liverwort; horehound, fine lavender, hyssop crops, pennyroyal, red fennel, of each of these one handful; of elecampane roots clean pared and sliced, two handfuls; then take all these aforesaid and shred them, but not wash them; then take four gallons and more of strong ale, and one gallon of sack lees, and put all these aforesaid herbs shred into it, and then put into it one pound of liquorice bruised, half a pound of aniseeds clean sifted and bruised, and of mace and nutmegs bruised of each one ounce; then put all together into your stilling-pot close covered with rye paste, and make a soft fire under your pot, and as the head of the limbeck

86

heateth, draw out your hot water and put in cold, keeping the head of your limbeck still with cold water, but see your fire be not too rash at the first, but let your water come at leisure, and take heed unto your stilling that your water change not white, for it is not so strong as the first draught is; and when the water is distilled, take a gallon glass with a wide mouth, and put therein a pottle of the best water and clearest, and put into it a pottle of *rosa solis*, half a pound of dates bruised, and one ounce of grains, half a pound of sugar, half an ounce of seed pearl beaten, three leaves of fine gold; stir all these together well, then stop your glass and set it in the run the space of one or two months, and then clarify it and use it at your discretion, for a spoonful or two at a time is sufficient, and the virtues are infinite.

Another excellent aqua vitae.

Fill a pot with red wine clean and strong, and put therein the powders of camomile, gillyflowers, ginger, pellitory, nutmeg, galingale, spikenard, quenebits, grains of pure long pepper, black pepper, cumin, fennel seed, smallage, parsley, sage, rue, mint, calamint, and horseshoe, of each of them a like quantity, and beware they differ not the weight of a dram under or above; then put all the powders above said into the wine, and after put them into the distilling pot, and distil it with a soft fire, and look that it be well luted about with rye paste, so that no fume or breath go forth, and look that the fire be temperate; also receive the water out of the limbeck into a glass vial. This water is called the water of life, and it may be likened to balm, for it hath all the virtues and properties which balm hath; this water is clear and lighter than rose-water, for it will fleet above all liquors, for if oil be put above this water, it sinketh to the bottom. This water keepeth flesh and fish, both raw and sodden, in his own kind and state, it is good against aches in the bones, the pox, and such like, neither can anything kept in this water rot or putrify; it doth draw out the sweetness, savour, and virtues of all manner of spices, roots and herbs that are wet or laid therein; it gives sweetness to all manner of water that is mixed with it; it is good for all manner of cold sicknesses, and namely for the palsy or trembling joints, and stretching of the sinews; it is good against the cold gout; and it maketh an old man seem young, using to drink it fasting; and lastly it fretteth away dead flesh in wounds, and killeth the canker.

To make aqua composita.

Take rosemary, thyme, hyssop, sage, fennel, nep, roots of elecampane, of each a handful, of marjoram, and pennyroyal of each half a handful; eight slips of red mint, half a pound of liquorice, half a pound of aniseeds, and two gallons of the best ale that can be brewed; wash all these herbs clean, and put the ale, liquorice, aniseeds, and herbs into a clean brass pot, and set your limbeck thereon, and paste it round about that no air come out, then distil the water with a gentle fire, and keep the limbeck cool above, not suffering it to run too fast; and take heed when your water changeth colour to put another glass under, and keep the first water, for it is most precious, and the latter water keep by itself, and put it into your next pot, and that shall make it much better.

To make the imperial water.

Take a gallon of Gascon wine; ginger, galingale, nutmegs, grains, cloves, aniseeds, fennel seeds, caraway seeds, of each one dram, then take sage, mints, red roses, thyme, pellitory, rosemary, wild thyme, camomile, and lavender, of each a handful, then bray the spices small, and the herbs also, and put all together into the wine, and let it stand so twelve hours, stirring it divers times, then distil it with a limbeck, and keep the first water, for it is best: of a gallon of wine you must not take above a quart of water; this water comforteth the vital spirits, and helpeth inward diseases that cometh of cold, as the palsy, the contraction of sinews; also it killeth worms, and comforts the stomach; it cureth the cold dropsy, helps the stone, the stinking breath, and maketh one seem young.

To make cinnamon water.

Take a pottle of the best sack, and half a pint of rose-water, a quarter and half of a pound of good cinnamon well bruised, but not small beaten; distil all these together in a glass still, but you must carefully look to it that it boil not over hastily, and attend it with cold wet cloths to cool the top of the still if the water should offer to boil too hastily. This water is very sovereign for the stomach, the head, and all the inward parts; it helps digestion, and comforteth the vital spirits.

*Six most precious waters, which Hippocrates made, and
sent to a queen sometime living in England.*

1. Take fennel, rue, vervain, endive, betony, germander,
red rose, *capillus veneris*, of each an ounce; stamp them
and steep them in white wine a day and a night, and
distil water of them, which water will divide in three
parts; the first water you shall put in a glass by itself, for
it is more precious than gold, the second as silver, and
the third as balm, and keep these three parts in glasses:
this water you shall give the rich for gold, to meaner for
silver, to poor men for balm: this water keepeth the sight
in clearness, and purgeth all gross humours.

2. Take *sal gemma* a pound, and lap it in a green dock
leaf, and lay it in the fire till it be well roasted, and wax
white, and put it in a glass against the air a night, and on
the morrow it shall be turned to a white water like unto
crystal: keep this water well in a glass, and put a drop into
the eye, and it shall cleanse and sharp the sight: it is good
for any evil at the heart, for the morphew, and the canker
of the mouth, and for divers other evils in the body.

3. Take the roots of fennel, parsley, endive, betony, of
each an ounce, and first wash them well in lukewarm
water, and bray them well [and steep them] with white
wine a day and a night, and then distil them into water:
this water is more worthy than balm; it preserveth the
sight much, and cleanseth it of all filth, it restraineth
tears, and comforteth the head, and avoideth the water
that cometh through the pain in the head.

4. Take the seed of parsley, achannes, vervain, cara-
ways and centaury, of each ten drams; beat all these

together, and put it in warm water a day and a night, and put it in a vessel to distil: this water is a precious water for all sore eyes, and very good for the health of man or woman's body.

5. Take limail of gold, silver, latten, copper, iron, steel, and lead; and take litharge of gold and silver; take calamint and columbine, and steep all together, the first day in the urine of a man child, that is between a day and a night, the second day in white wine, the third day in the juice of fennel, the fourth day in the whites of eggs, the fifth day in the woman's milk that nourisheth a man child, the sixth day in red wine, the seventh day in the whites of eggs, and upon the eighth day bind all these together, and distil the water of them, and keep this water in a vessel of gold or silver: the virtues of this water are these, first it expelleth all rheums, and doth away all manner of sickness from the eyes, and wears away the pearl, pin, and web; it draweth again into his own kind the eyelids that have been bleared, it easeth the ache of the head, and, if a man drink it, maketh him look young even in old age, besides a world of other most excellent virtues.

6. Take the goldsmith's stone, and put it into the fire, till it be red hot, and quench it in a pint of white wine, and do so nine times, and after grind it, and beat it small, and cleanse it as clean as you may, and after set it in the sun with the water of fennel distilled, and vervain, roses, celandine, and rue, and a little aqua vitae, and when you have sprinkled it in the water nine times, put it then in a vessel of glass, and yet upon a reversion of the water distil it, till it pass over the touch four or five inches; and

when you will use it then stir it all together, and then take up a drop with a feather, and put it on your nail, and if it abide, it is fine and good: then put it in the eye that runneth, or anoint the head with it if it ache, and the temples; and believe it, that of all waters this is the most precious, and helpeth the sight or any pain in the head.

The virtues of several waters.

The water of chervil is good for a sore mouth.

The water of calamint is good for the stomach.

The water of plantain is good for the flux, and the hot dropsy.

Water of fennel is good to make a fat body small, and also for the eyes.

Water of violets is good for a man that is sore within his body, and for the reins, and for the liver.

Water of endive is good for the dropsy, and for the jaundice, and the stomach.

Water of borage is good for the stomach, and for the *iliaca passio*, and many other sicknesses in the body.

Water of both sages is good for the palsy.

Water of betony is good for the hearing and all inward sicknesses.

Water of radish drunk twice a day, at each time an ounce, or an ounce and a half, doth multiply and provoke lust, and also it provoketh the terms in women.

Rosemary water (the face washed therein both morning and night) causeth a fair and clear countenance: also the head washed therewith, and let dry of itself, preserveth the falling of the hair, and causeth more to grow; also two ounces of the same, drunk, driveth venom out of the body in the same sort as mithridate doth; the same twice or thrice drunk, at each time half an ounce, rectifieth the mother, and it causeth women to be fruitful: when one maketh a bath of this decoction, it is called the bath of life; the same drunk comforteth the heart, the brain, and the whole body, and cleanseth away the spots of the face; it maketh a man look young, and causeth women to conceive quickly, and hath all the virtues of balm.

Water of rue drunk in a morning four or five days together, at each time an ounce, purifieth the flowers in women; the same water, drunk in the morning fasting, is good against the griping of the bowels, and, drunk at morning and at night, at each time an ounce, it provoketh the terms in women.

The water of sorrel drunk is good for all burning and pestilent fevers, and all other hot sicknesses; being mixed with beer, ale, or wine, it slaketh thirst; it is also good for the yellow jaundice, being taken six or eight days together; it also expelleth heat from the liver if it be drunk and a cloth wet in the same and a little wrung out, and so applied to the right side over against the liver, and when it is dry then wet another, and apply it; and thus do three or four times together.

Lastly the water of angelica is good for the head, for inward infection, either of the plague or pestilence; it is very sovereign for sore breasts; also the same water, being drunk of twelve or thirteen days together, is good to unlade the stomach of gross humours and superfluities, and it strengtheneth and comforteth all the universal parts of the body: and lastly, it is a most sovereign medicine for the gout, by bathing the diseased members much therein.

Now to conclude. It is meet that our housewife know that from the eight of the calends of the month of April unto the eight of the calends of July, all manner of herbs and leaves are in that time most in strength and of the greatest virtue to be used and put in all manner of medicines; also from the eight of the calends of July unto the eight of the calends of October the stalks, stems, and hard branches of every herb and plant is most in strength to be used in medicines; and from the eight of the calends of October, unto the eight of the calends of April, all manner of roots of herbs and plants are the most of strength and virtue to be used in all manner of medicines.

To make vinegar.

To make excellent strong vinegar, you shall brew the strongest ale that may be, and having tunned it in a very strong vessel, you shall set it either in your garden or some other safe place abroad, where it may have the whole summer day's sun to shine upon it, and there let it lie till it be extreme sour, then into a hogshead of this vinegar put the leaves of four or five hundred damask roses, and after they have lain for the space of a month therein, house the vinegar and draw it as you need it.

To make dry vinegar.

To make dry vinegar which you may carry in your pocket, you shall take the blades of green corn, either wheat or rye, and beat it in a mortar with the strongest vinegar you can get till it come to a paste; then roll it into little balls, and dry it in the sun till it be very hard; then when you have any occasion to use it, cut a little piece thereof and dissolve it in wine, and it will make a strong vinegar.

To make verjuice.

To make verjuice, you shall gather your crabs as soon as the kernels turn black, and, having laid them a while in a heap to sweat together, take them and pick them from stalks, blacks, and rottenness: then in long troughs with beetles for the purpose, crush and break them all to mash: then make a bag of coarse haircloth as square as the press, and fill it with the crushed crabs; then put it into the press, and press it while any moisture will drop forth, having a clean vessel underneath to receive the liquor: this done, tun it up into sweet hogsheads, and to every hogshead put half a dozen handfuls of damask rose leaves, and then bung it up, and spend it as you shall have occasion.

Many other pretty secrets there are belonging unto curious housewives, but none more necessary than these already rehearsed, except such as shall hereafter follow in their proper places.

How to make sweet water.

Take of bay leaves one handful, of red roses two handfuls, of damask roses three handful, of lavender four hand-fuls, of basil one handful, marjoram two handfuls, of camomile one handful, the young tops of sweet briar two handfuls, of dandelion [and] tansy two handfuls, of orange peels six or seven ounces, of cloves and mace a groat's worth: put all these together in a pottle of new ale in corns for the space of three days, shaking it every day three or four times; then distil it the fourth day in a still with a continual soft fire, and, after it is distilled, put into it a grain or two of musk.

A very rare and pleasant damask water.

Take a quart of malmsey lees, or a quart of malmsey simply, one handful of marjoram, of basil as much, of lavender four handfuls, bay leaves one good handful, damask rose leaves four handfuls, and as many of red, the peels of six oranges, or for want of them one handful of the tender leaves of walnut trees, of benjamin half an ounce, of *calamus aromaticus* as much, of camphor four drams, of cloves one ounce, of *labdanum* half an ounce; then take a pottle of running water, and put in all these spices bruised into your water and malmsey together in a close stopped pot, with a good handful of rosemary, and let them stand for the space of six days; then distil it with a soft fire; then set it in the sun sixteen days with four grains of musk bruised. This quantity will make three quarts of water. *Probatum est.*

The ordering, preserving, and helping
of all sorts of wines

I do not assume to myself this knowledge of the vintner's secrets, but ingeniously confess that one professed skilful in the trade, having rudely written, and more rudely disclosed this secret, and preferring it to the stationer, it came to me to be polished, which I have done, knowing that it is necessary, etc.

It is necessary that our English housewife be skilful in the election, preservation, and curing of all sorts of wines, because they be usual charges under her hands, and by the least neglect must turn the husband to much loss: therefore to speak first of the election of sweet wines, she must be careful that her malmseys be full wines, pleasant, well hued, and fine: that bastard be fat, and if it be tawny it skills not, for the tawny bastards be always the sweetest. Muscadine must be great, pleasant, and strong, with a sweet scent, and with amber colour. Sack if it be Seres (as it should be) you shall know it by the mark of a cork burned on one side of the bung, and they be ever full gauge, and so are no other sacks, and the longer they lie, the better they be.

To make muscadine, and give it a flavour.

Take a pleasant butt of malmsey, and draw it out a quarter and more; then fill it up with fat bastard within eight gallons, or thereabouts, and parel it with six eggs, yolks and all, one handful of bay salt, and a pint of conduit water to every parel, and if the wine be high of colour, put in three gallons of new milk, but skim off the cream first, and beat it well: or otherwise if you have a good butt of malmsey, and a good pipe of bastard, you must take some empty butt or pipe, and draw thirty gallons of malmsey, and as many of bastard, and beat them well together; and when you have so done, take a quarter of a pound of ginger and bruise it, and put it into your vessel; then fill it up with malmsey and bastard: or otherwise thus; if you have a pleasant butt of malmsey, which is called ralt-mow, you may draw out of it forty gallons, and if your bastard be very faint, then thirty gallons of it will serve to make it pleasant; then take four gallons of new milk and beat it, and put it into it when it lacketh twelve gallons of full, and then make your flavour.

How to flavour muscadine.

Take one ounce of corianders, of bay salt, of cloves, of each as much, one handful of savory; let all these be blended and bruised together, and sew them close in a bag, and take half a pint of damask water and lay your flavour into it, and then put it into your butt, and if it [will not] fine, give it a parel and fill it up, and let it lie till it fine: or else thus; take coriander roots a pennyworth, one pound of aniseeds, one pennyworth in ginger; bruise them together and put them into a bag as before, and make your bag long and small that it may go in and out at the bung hole, and when you do put it in, fasten it with a thread at the bung; then take a pint of the strongest damask water, and warm it lukewarm, then put it into the butt, and then stop it close for two or three days at least, and then if you please you may set it abroach.

To parel muscadine when it comes new in to be fined in twenty-four hours.

Take seven whites of new laid eggs, two handfuls of bay salt, and beat them well together, and put therein a pint of sack or more, and beat them till they be as short as snow; then overdraw the butt seven or eight gallons, and beat the wine, and stir the lees, and then put in the parel and beat it, and so fill it up, and stop it close, and draw it on the morrow.

To make white bastard.

Draw out of a pipe of bastard ten gallons, and put to it five gallons of new milk, and skim it as before, and all to beat it with a parel of eight whites of eggs, and a handful of bay salt, and a pint of conduit water, and it will be white and fine in the morning. But if you will make very fine bastard, take a white wine hogshead, and put out the lees, and wash it clean, and fill it half full and half a quarter, and put to it four gallons of new milk and beat it well with the whites of six eggs, and fill it up with white wine and sack, and it will be white and fine.

How to help bastard being eager.

Take two gallons of the best stoned honey, and two gallons of white wine, and boil them in a fair pan; skim it clean, and strain it through a fair cloth that there be no motes in it: then put to it one ounce of corianders, and one ounce of aniseeds, four or five orange peels dry and beaten to powder, let them lie three days; then draw your bastard into a clean pipe, then put in your honey with the rest, and beat it well; then let it lie a week and touch it not, after draw it at pleasure.

To make bastard white, and to rid away lags.

If your bastard be fat and good, draw out forty gallons, then may you fill it up with the lags of any kind of white wines or sacks; then take five gallons of new milk, and first take away the cream, then strain it through a clean cloth, and when your pipe is three quarters full, put in your milk; then beat it very well, and fill it so that it may lack fifteen gallons, then parel it thus: take the whites only of ten eggs, and beat them in a fair tray with bay salt and conduit water; then put it into the pipe and beat it well, and so fill it up, and let it stand open all night; and if you will keep it any while, you must on the morrow stop it close; and to make the same drink like osey, give it this flavour: take a pound of aniseeds, two pence in corianders, two pence in ginger, two pence in cloves, two pence in grains, two pence in long pepper, and two pence in liquorice: bruise all these together; then make two bags of linen cloth, long and small, and put your spices into them, and put them into the pipe at the bung, making them fast there with a thread that it may sink into the wine; then stop it close, and in two days you may broach it.

A remedy for bastard if it prick.

Take and draw him from his lees if he have any, and put the wine into a malmsey butt to the lees of malmsey;

then put to the bastard that is in the malmsey butt nigh three gallons of the best wort of a fresh tap, and then fill him up with bastard or malmsey or cuit if you will: then parel it thus; first, parel him, and beat him with a staff, and then take the whites of four new laid eggs, and beat them with a handful of salt till it be short as moss, and then put a pint of running water therein, and so fill the pipe up full, and lay a tile stone on the bung, and set it abroach within four and twenty hours if you will.

To make malmsey.

If you have a good butt of malmsey, and a butt or two of sack that will not be drunk: for the sack prepare some empty butt or pipe, and draw it more than half full of sack, then fill it up with malmsey, and when your butt is full within a little, put into it three gallons of Spanish cuit, the best that you can get, then beat it well, then take your taster and see that it be deep coloured; then fill it up with sack, and give it a parel, and beat it well: the parel is thus; take the yolks of ten eggs and beat them in a clean basin with a handful of bay salt, and a quart of conduit water, and beat them together with a little piece of birch, and beat it till it be as short as moss; then draw five or six gallons out of your butt, then beat it again, and then fill it up, and the next day it will be ready to be drawn. This parel will serve both for muscadine, bastard and for sack.

To shift malmsey, and to rid away ill wines.

If you have two principal butts of malmsey, you may make three good butts with your lags of claret and of sack: if you put two gallons of red wine in a butt, it will save the more cuit; then put two or three gallons of cuit as you see cause; and if it be Spanish cuit, two gallons will go further than five gallons of Candy cuit, but the Candy cuit is more natural for the malmsey: also one butt of good malmsey, and a butt of sack that hath lost his colour, will make two good butts of malmsey with the more cuit; and when you have filled your butts within twelve gallons, then put in your cuit, and beat it half an hour and more; then put in your parel and let it lie.

If sack want his colour.

First, parel him as you did the bastard, and order him as shall be showed you for the white wine of Gascony with milk, and so set him abroach.

For sack that is tawny.

If your sack have a strong lee or taste, take a good sweet butt fair washed, and draw your sack into it, and make unto it a parel as you do to the bastard, and beat it very well, and so stop up your butt: and if it be tawny, take three gallons of new milk, and strain it clean, and put it into your sack, then beat it very well, and stop it close.

For sack that doth rope and is brown.

Take a fair empty butt with the lees in it, and draw your sack into the same from his lees fine; then take a pound of rice flour as fine as you can get, and four grains of camphor, and put it into the sack; and if it will not fine, give it a good parel, and beat it well; then stop it and let it lie.

To colour sack, or any white wine.

If any of your sacks or white wines have lost their colour, take three gallons of new milk, and take away the cream; then overdraw your wine five or six gallons, then put in your milk and beat it; then lay it aforetake all night, and in the morning lay it up, and the next day if you will you may set it abroach.

If alicant be grown hard.

Draw him out into fresh lees, and take three or four gallons of stone honey clarified, and, being cool, put it in and parel it with the yolks of four eggs, whites and all, and beat it well, and fill it up, and stop it close, and it will be pleasant and quick as long as it is in drawing.

For alicant that is sour.

Take three gallons of white honey, and two gallons of red wine, boil them together in a fair pan, and skim it clean, and let it stand till it be fine and cold, then put it into your pipe; yet nothing but the finest; then beat it well, and fill it up, and stop it close, and if your alicant be pleasant and great, it will do much good, for the one pipe will rid away divers.

How to order Rhenish wine.

There are two sorts of Rhenish wines, that is to say, Elstertune and Brabant: the Elstertune are best, you shall know it by the vat, for it is double barred and double pinned; the Brabant is nothing so good, and there is not so much good to be done with them as with the other. If the wines be good and pleasant, a man may rid away a hogshead or two of white wine, and this is the most vantage a man can have by them: and if it be slender and hard, then take three or four gallons of stone honey and clarify it clean; then put into the honey four or five gallons of the same wine, and then let it seethe a great while, and put into it two pence in cloves bruised; let them seethe together, for it will take away the scent of honey, and when it is sodden take it off, and set it by till it be thorough cold; then take four gallons of milk and order it as before, and then put all into your wine and all to beat it; and (if you can) roll it, for that is the best way; then stop it close and let it lie, and that will make it pleasant.

Of what countries wines are by their names.

The wines that be made in Bordeaux are called Gascon wines, and you shall know them by their hazel hoops, and the most be full gauge and sound wines.

The wines of the high countries, and which is called high country wine, are made some thirty or forty miles beyond Bordeaux, and they come not down so soon as the other; for if they do, they are all forfeited; and you shall know them ever by their hazel hoops, and the length gauge lacks.

Then you have wines that be called Gallaway both in pipes and hogsheads, and be long, and lacks two sesters and a half in gauge, and the wines themselves are high coloured. Then there are other whites which is called white wine of Angulle, very good wine, and lacks little of gauge, and that is also in pipes for the most part, and is quarter bound. Then there are Rochelle wines, which are also in pipes long and slender; they are very small hedge wines, sharp in taste, and of a pallid complexion. Our best sack are of Seres in Spain, your smaller of Galicia and Portugal; your strong sacks are of the islands of the Canaries, and of Malaga; and your muscadines and malmseys are of many parts of Italy, Greece, and some especial islands.

Of Gascon wines.

See that in your choice of Gascon wines you observe that your claret wines be fair coloured, and bright as a ruby, not deep as an amethyst; for though it may show strength, yet it wants neatness: also let it be sweet as a rose or a violet, and in any case let it be short; for if it be long, then in no wise meddle with it.

For your white wines, see they be sweet and pleasant at the nose, very short, clear and bright and quick in the taste.

Lastly for your red wine, provide that they be deep coloured and pleasant, long, and sweet, and if in them or claret wines be any default of colour, there are remedies enough to amend and repair them.

To remedy claret wine that hath lost his colour.

If your claret wine be faint, and have lost his colour; then take a fresh hogshead with his fresh lees which was very good wine, and draw your wine into the same; then stop it close and tight, and lay it aforetake for two or three days that the lees may run through it, then lay it up till it be fine, and if the colour be not perfect, draw it into a red wine hogshead, that is new drawn with the lees, and that will colour of himself, and make him strong; or take a pound of turnsole or two, and beat it with a gallon or two of wine, and let it lie a day or two, then put it into your hogshead, draw your wine again, and wash your cloths, then lay it aforetake all night, and roll it on the morrow; then lay it up, and it will have a perfect colour.

A remedy for Gascon wine that hath lost his colour.

And if your claret wine have lost his colour, take a pennyworth of damsons, or else black bullaces, as you see cause, and stew them with some red wine of the deepest colour, and make thereof a pound or more of syrup, and put it into a clean glass, and after into the hogshead of claret wine; and the same you may likewise do unto red wine if you please.

For white wine that have lost his colour.

Take three gallons of new milk, and take away the cream off it; then draw five or six gallons of wine, and put your milk into the hogshead, and beat it exceeding well; then fill it up; but before you fill it up, if you can, roll it, and if it be long and small, take half a pound of roche alum finely beaten into powder, and put into the vessel, and let it lie.

A remedy for white wine that hath lost his colour.

And if your white wine be faint, and have lost his colour, if the wine have any strength in it; take to a hogshead so much as you intend to put in, out of the said milk, and a handful of rice beaten very well, and a little salt, and lay him aforetake all night, and on the morning lay him up again, and set it abroach in any wise the next wine you spend, for it will not last long.

A remedy for claret, or white wine that drinks foul.

Take and draw it into new lees of the one nature, and then take a dozen of new pippins, and pare them, and take away the cores, and then put them in, and if that will not serve, take a handful of the oak of Jerusalem, and stamp it, then put it into your wine, and beat it exceedingly well, and it will not only take away the foulness, but also make it have a good scent at the nose.

For red wine that drinks faint.

If your red wine drink faint, then take a hogshead that alicant hath been in with the lees also, and draw your wine into it, and that will refresh it well, and make the wine well coloured; or otherwise draw it close to fresh lees, and that will recover it again, and put to it three or four gallons of alicant, and turn it on his lees.

For red wine that wants colour.

If your red wine lack colour, then take out four gallons, and put in four gallons of alicant, and turn him on his lees, and the bung up, and his colour will return, and be fair.

Of the excellency of oats

Oats, although they are of all manner of grain the cheapest because of their generality, being a grain of that goodness and hardness that it will grow in any soil whatsoever, be it never so rich or never so poor, as if nature had made it the only loving companion and true friend to mankind, yet is it a grain of that singularity for the multiplicity of virtues, and necessary uses for the sustenance and support of the family, that not any other grain is to be compared with it; for if any other have equal virtue, yet it hath not equal value, and if equal value, then it wants many degrees of equal virtue: so that joining virtue and value together, no husband, housewife, or house-keeper whatsoever hath so true and worthy a friend as his oats are.

Virtue of oats to cattle.

To speak then first of the virtues of oats, as they accrue to cattle and creatures without door, and first to begin with the horse; there is not any food whatsoever that is so good, wholesome, and agreeable with the nature of a horse as oats are, being a provender in which he taketh such delight, that with it he feedeth, travaileth and doth any violent labour whatsoever with more courage and comfort than with any other food that can be invented, as all men know that have either use of it, or horses; neither doth the horse ever take surfeit of oats (if they be sweet and dry), for albeit he may well be glutted or stalled upon them (with indiscreet feeding) and so refuse them for a little time, yet he never surfeiteth, or any present sickness followeth after; whereas no other grain but glut a horse therewith, and instantly sickness will follow, which shows surfeit, and the danger is oft incurable: for we read in Italy, at the seige of Naples, of many hundred horses that died on the surfeit of wheat; at Rome also died many hundred horses of the plague, which by due proof was found to proceed from a surfeit taken of pease and vetches; and so I could run over all other grains, but it is needless, and far from the purpose I have to handle: suffice it, oats for horses are the best of all foods whatsoever, whether they be but only clean threshed from the straw, and so dried, or converted to oatmeal, and so ground and made into bread; oats boiled and given to a horse whilst they are cool and sweet are an excellent food for any horse in the time of disease, poverty, or sickness, for they scour and fat exceedingly.

In the same nature that oats are for horses, so are they for the ass, mule, camel, or any other beast of burden.

If you will feed either ox, bull, cow, or any neat whatsoever to an extraordinary height of fatness, there is no food doth it so soon as oats doth, whether you give them in the straw, or clean threshed from the sheaf, and well winnowed; but the winnowed oat is the best, for by them I have seen an ox fed to twenty pound, to twenty-four pound, and thirty pounds, which is a most unreasonable reckoning for any beast, only fame and the tallow hath been precious.

For sheep, goats, swine, and hounds.

Sheep or goats may likewise be fed with oats, to as great price and profit as with pease, and swine are fed with oats, either in raw malt, or otherwise, to as great thickness as with any grain whatsoever; only they must have a few pease after the oats to harden the fat, or else it will waste, and consume in boiling. Now for holding swine, which are only to be preserved in good flesh, nothing is better than a thin mange made of ground oats, whey, buttermilk, or other ordinary wash or swillings which either the dairy or kitchen affordeth; nor is there any more sovereign or excellent meat for swine in the time of sickness, than a mange made of ground oats and sweet whey, warmed lukewarm on the fire and mixed with the powder of raddle, or red ochre. Nay, if you will go to the matter of pleasure, there is not any meat so excellent for the feeding and wholesome keeping of a kennel of hounds, as the mange made of ground oats and scalding water, or of beef broth, or any other broth in which flesh hath been sodden; if it be for the feeding, strengthening, and comforting of greyhounds, spaniels, or any other sort of tenderer dogs, there is no meat better than sheep's heads, hair and all, or other entrails of sheep chopped and well sodden, with good store of oatmeal.

For poultry.

Now for all manner of poultry, as cocks, capons, chickens of great size, turkeys, geese, ducks, swans, and such

like, there is no food feedeth them better than oats, and
if it be the young breed of any of those kinds, even from
the first hatching or disclosing, till they be able to shift
for themselves, there is no food better whatsoever than
oatmeal grits, or fine oatmeal, either simple of itself, or
else mixed with milk, drink, or else new made urine.

Virtue of oats.

Thus much touching the virtues and quality of oats or
oatmeal, as they are serviceable for the use of cattle and
poultry. Now for the most necessary use thereof for man,
and the general support of the family, there as no grain
in our knowledge answerable unto it; first, for the simple
oat itself (excepting some particular physic helps,
as frying them with sweet butter, and putting them in
a bag, and very hot applied to the belly or stomach to
avoid colic or windiness, and such like experiments) the
most especial use which is made of them is for malt to
make beer or ale of which it doth exceeding well, and
maintaineth many towns and countries; but the oatmeal
which is drawn from them, being the heart and kernel of
the oat, is a thing of much rarer price and estimation; for
to speak troth, it is, like salt, of such a general use that
without it hardly can any family be maintained:

Making of oatmeal.

therefore I think it not much amiss to speak a word or
two touching the making of oatmeal: you shall understand
then that to make good and perfect oatmeal you shall
first dry your oats exceeding well, and then put them on
the mill, which may either be water-mill, wind-mill, or

horse-mill (but the horse-mill is best) and no more but crush or hull them; that is, to carry the stones so large that they may no more but crush the husk from the kernel: then you shall winnow the hulls from the kernels either with the wind or a fan, and finding them of an indifferent cleanness (for it is impossible to hull them all clean at the first) you shall then put them on again, and, making the mill go a little closer, run them through the mill again, and then winnow them over again, and such grits or kernels as are clean hulled and well cut you may lay by, and the rest you shall run through the mill again the third time, and so winnow them again, in which time all will be perfect, and the grits or full kernels will separate from the smaller oatmeal; for you shall understand that at this first making of oatmeal you shall ever have two sorts of oatmeals; that is, the full whole grit or kernel, and the small dust oatmeal: as for the coarse hulls or chaff that cometh from them, that also is worthy saving, for it is an excellent good horse provender for any plow or labouring horses, being mixed with either beans, pease, or any other pulse whatsoever.

The virtues of oatmeal.

Now for the use and virtues of these two several kinds of oatmeals in maintaining the family, they are so many (according to the many customs of many nations) that it is almost impossible to reckon all; yet (as near as I can) I will impart my knowledge, and what I have ta'en from relation: first, for the small dust or meal oatmeal, it is that with which all pottage is made and thickened, whether they be meat pottage, milk pottage, or any thick

112

or else thin gruel whatsoever, of whose goodness and wholesomeness it is needless to speak, in that it is frequent with every experience: also with this small oatmeal is made in divers countries six several kinds of very good and wholesome bread, every one finer than other, as your anacks, janacks, and such like. Also there is made of it both thick and thin oaten cakes, which are very pleasant in taste, and much esteemed: but if it be mixed with fine wheat meal, then it maketh a most delicate and dainty oatcake, either thick or thin, such as no prince in the world but may have them served to his table; also this small oatmeal mixed with blood, and the liver of either sheep, calf or swine, maketh that pudding which is called the haggas or haggus, of whose goodness it is in vain to boast, because there is hardly to be found a man that doth not affect them. And lastly from this small oatmeal, by oft steeping it in water and cleansing it, and then boiling it to a thick and stiff jelly, is made that excellent dish of meat, which is so esteemed in the west parts of this kingdom, which they call washbrew, and in Cheshire and Lancashire they call it flammery or flummery, the wholesomeness and rare goodness, nay the very physic helps thereof being such and so many that I myself have heard a very reverend and worthily renowned physician speak more in the commendation of that meat than of any other food whatsoever: and certain it is that you shall not hear of any that ever did surfeit of this washbrew or flummery; and yet I have seen them of very dainty and sickly stomachs which have eaten great quantities thereof, beyond the proportion of ordinary meats. Now for the manner of eating this meat, it is of divers diversely used; for some eat it with honey, which is reputed the best sauce; some with wine, either sack, claret or white; some with strong beer or strong ale, and some with milk, as your ability, or the accommodations of the place will administer. Now there is derived from this washbrew another coarser meat, which is as it were the dregs or grosser substance of the washbrew, which is called girtbrew, which is a well filling and sufficient meat, fit for servants and men of labour; of the commendations whereof, I will not much stand, in that it is a meat of harder digestion, and fit indeed but for strong able stomachs, and such whose toil and much sweat both liberally spendeth evil humours, and also preserveth men from the offence of fullness and surfeits.

Of oatmeal grits.

Now for the bigger kind of oatmeal, which is called grits, or corn oatmeal, it is of no less use than the former, nor are there fewer meats compounded thereof: for first, of these grits are made all sorts of puddings, or pots (as the West Country terms them) whether they be black, as those which are made of the blood of beasts, swine, sheep, geese, red or fallow deer, or the like, mixed with whole grits, suet, and wholesome herbs: or else white, as when the grits are mixed with good cream, eggs, bread crumbs, suet, currants, and other wholesome spices. Also of these grits are made the Good Friday pudding, which is mixed with eggs, milk, suet, pennyroyal, and boiled first in a linen bag, and then stripped and buttered with sweet butter. Again, if you roast a goose, and stop her belly with whole grits, beaten together with eggs, and after mixed with the gravy, there cannot be a better or more pleasanter sauce: nay, if a man be at sea in any long travel, he cannot eat a more wholesome and pleasant meat than these whole grits boiled in water till they burst, and then mixed with butter, and so eaten with spoons; which although seamen call simply by the name of loblolly, yet there is not any meat how significant soever the name be, that is more toothsome or wholesome. And to conclude, there is no way or purpose whatsoever to which a man can use or employ rice, but with the same seasoning and order you may employ the whole grits of oatmeal, and have full as good and wholesome meat, and as well tasted: so that I may well knit up this chapter with this approbation of oatmeal, that the little charge and great benefit considered, it is the very crown of the housewife's garland, and doth more grace her table and her knowledge, than all grains whatsoever; neither indeed can any family or household be well and thriftily maintained, where this is either scant or wanting. And thus much touching the nature, worth, virtues, and great necessity of oats and oatmeal.

Of the brew-house and the bake-house

Of bread and drink.

When our English housewife knows how to preserve health by wholesome physic; to nourish by good meat, and to clothe the body with warm garments, she must not then by any means be ignorant in the provision of bread and drink; she must know both the proportions and compositions of the same. And forasmuch as drink is in every house more generally spent than bread, being indeed (but how well I know not) made the very substance of all entertainment, I will first begin with it;

Diversities of drinks.

and therefore you shall know that generally our kingdom hath but two kinds of drinks, that is to say, beer and ale, but particularly four, as beer, ale, perry, and cider; and to these we may add two more, mead and metheglin, two compound drinks of honey and herbs, which in the places where they are made, as in Wales and the Marches, are reckoned for exceeding wholesome and cordial.

Strong beer.

To speak then of beer, although there be divers kinds of tastes and strength thereof, according to the allowance

116

of malt, hops, and age given unto the same; yet indeed there can be truly said to be but two kinds thereof; namely, ordinary beer and March beer, all other beers being derived from them.

Of ordinary beer.

Touching ordinary beer, which is that wherewith either nobleman, gentleman, yeoman, or husbandman shall maintain his family the whole year; it is meet first that our English housewife respect the proportion or allowance of malt due to the same, which amongst the best husbands is thought most convenient, and it is held that to draw from one quarter of good malt three hogsheads of beer is the best ordinary proportion that can be allowed, and having age and good cask to lie in, it will be strong enough for any goodman's drinking.

Of brewing ordinary beer.

Now for the brewing of ordinary beer, your malt being well ground and put in your mash vat, and your liquor in your lead ready to boil, you shall then by little and little with scoops or pails put the boiling liquor to the malt, and then stir it even to the bottom exceedingly well together (which is called the mashing of the malt) then, the liquor swimming in the top, cover all over with more malt, and so let it stand an hour and more in the mash vat, during which space you may if you please heat more liquor in your lead for your second or small drink; this done, pluck up your mashing strom, and let the first liquor run gently from the malt, either in a clean trough or other vessels prepared for the purpose, and then stopping the mash vat again, put the second liquor to the malt and stir it well together; then your lead being emptied put your first liquor or wort therein, and then to every quarter of malt put a pound and a half of the best hops you can get, and boil them an hour together, till taking up a dishful thereof you see the hops shrink into the bottom of the dish; this done, put the wort through a straight sieve, which may drain the hops from it, into your cooler, which, standing over the gyle vat, you shall in the bottom thereof set a great bowl with your barm and some of the first wort (before the hops come into it) mixed together, that it may rise therein, and then let your wort drop or run gently into the dish with the barm which stands in the gyle vat; and this you shall do the first day of your brewing, letting your cooler drop all the night following, and some part of the next morning, and as it droppeth if you find that a black scum or mother riseth upon the barm, you shall with your hand take it off and cast it away; then nothing being left in the cooler, and the beer well risen, with your hand stir it about and so let it stand an hour after, and then, beating it and the barm exceeding well together, tun it up into the hogsheads being clean washed and scalded, and so let it purge: and herein you shall observe not to tun your vessels too full, for fear thereby it purge too much of the barm away: when it hath purged a day and a night, you shall close up the bung holes with clay, and only for a day or two after keep a vent-hole in it, and after close it up as close as may be.

Of small beer.

Now for your second or small drink which are left upon the grains, you shall suffer it there to stay but an hour or a little better and then drain it off also; which done, put it into the lead with the former hops and boil the other also, then clear it from the hops and cover it very close till your first beer be tunned, and then as before put it also to barm and so tun it up also in smaller vessels, and of this second beer you shall not draw above one hogshead to three of the better. Now there be divers other ways and observations for the brewing of ordinary beer, but none so good, so easy, so ready, and quickly performed as this before showed: neither will any beer last longer or ripen sooner, for it may be drunk at a fortnight's age, and will last as long and lively.

Of brewing the best March beer.

Now for the brewing of the best March beer you shall allow to a hogshead thereof a quarter of the best malt well ground: then you shall take a peck of pease, half a peck of wheat, and half a peck of oats and grind them all very well together, and then mix them with your malt: which done, you shall in all points brew this beer as you did the former ordinary beer; only you shall allow a pound and a half of hops to this one hogshead: and whereas before you drew but two sorts of beer, so now you shall draw three; that is a hogshead of the best, and a hogshead of the second, and half a hogshead of small beer without any augmentation of hops or malt.

This March beer would be brewed in the months of March or April, and should (if it have right) lie a whole year to ripen: it will last two, three and four years if it lie cool and close, and endure the drawing to the last drop, though with never so much leisure.

Brewing of strong ale.

Now for the brewing of strong ale, because it is drink of no such long lasting as beer is, therefore you shall brew less quantity at a time thereof, as two bushels of northern measure (which is four bushels or half a quarter in the south) at a brewing, and not above, which will make fourteen gallons of the best ale. Now for the mashing and ordering of it in the mash vat, it will not differ anything from that of beer; as for hops, although some use not to put in any, yet the best brewers thereof will allow to fourteen gallons of ale a good espen full of hops, and no more; yet before you put in your hops, as soon as you take it from the grains you shall put it into a vessel and change it, or blink it in this manner: put into the wort a handful of oak boughs and a pewter dish, and let them lie therein till the wort look a little paler than it did at the first, and then presently take out the dish and the leaf, and then boil it a full hour with the hops as aforesaid, and then cleanse it, and set it in vessels to cool; when it is no more but milk warm, having set your barm to rise with some sweet wort, then put all into the gyle vat, and as soon as it riseth, with a dish or bowl beat it in, and so keep it with continual beating a day and a night at least, and after tun it. From this ale you may also draw half so much very good middle ale, and a third part very good small ale.

Brewing of bottle ale.

Touching the brewing of bottle ale, it differeth nothing at all from the brewing of strong ale, only it must be drawn in a larger proportion, as at least twenty gallons of half a quarter; and when it comes to be changed you shall blink it (as was before showed) more by much than was the strong ale, for it must be pretty and sharp, which giveth the life and quickness to the ale: and when you tun it, you shall put it into round bottles with narrow mouths, and then stopping them close with cork, set them in a cold cellar up to the waist in sand, and be sure that the corks be fast tied in with strong pack-thread, for fear of rising out, or taking vent, which is the utter spoil of the ale. Now for the small drink arising from this bottle ale, or any other beer or ale whatsoever, if you keep it after it is blinked and boiled in a close vessel, and then put it to barm every morning as you have occasion to use it, the drink will drink a great deal the fresher, and be much more lively in taste.

Of making perry or cider.

As for the making of perry and cider, which are drinks much used in the west parts, and other countries well stored with fruit in this kingdom; you shall know that your perry is made of pears only, and your cider of apples; and for the manner of making thereof, it is done after one fashion; that is to say, after your pears or apples are well picked from the stalks, rottenness, and all manner of other filth, you shall put them in the press mill which is made with a millstone running round in a circle, under which you shall crush your pears or apples, and then, straining them through a bag of haircloth, tun up the same, after it hath been a little settled, into hogsheads, barrels, and other close vessels.

Now after you have pressed all, you shall save that which is within the haircloth bag, and, putting it into several vessels, put a pretty quantity of water thereunto, and after it hath stood a day or two, and hath been well stirred together, press it over also again, for this will make a small perry or cider, and must be spent first. Now of your best cider, that which you make of your summer or sweet fruit, you shall call summer or sweet cider or perry, and that you shall spend first also; and that which you make of the winter and hard fruit you shall call winter and sour cider, or perry; and that you shall spend last, for it will endure the longest.

Of baking.

Thus after our English housewife is experienced in the brewing of these several drinks, she shall then look into her bakehouse, and to the baking of all sorts of bread, either for masters, servants, or hinds, and to the ordering and compounding of the meal for each several use.

Ordering of meal.

To speak then first of meals for bread, they are either simple or compound; simple as wheat and rye, or compound, as rye and wheat mixed together, or rye, wheat, and barley mixed together; and of these the oldest meal is ever the best, and yieldeth most so it be sweet and untainted; for the preservation whereof, it is meet that you cleanse your meal well from the bran, and then keep it in sweet vessels.

Of baking manchets.

Now for the baking of bread of your simple meals, your best and principal bread is manchet, which you shall bake in this manner; first your meal, being ground upon the black stones if it be possible, which makes the whitest flour, and bolted through the finest bolting cloth, you shall put it into a clean kimnel, and, opening the flour hollow in the midst, put into it of the best ale barm the quantity of three pints to a bushel of meal, with some salt to season it with: then put in your liquor reasonable warm and knead it very well together both with your hands and through the brake; or for want thereof, fold it in a cloth, and with your feet tread it a good space together, then, letting it lie an hour or thereabouts to swell, take it forth and mould it into manchets, round, and flat; scotch about the waist to give it leave to rise, and prick it with your knife in the top, and so put it into the oven, and bake it with a gentle heat.

Of baking cheat bread.

To bake the best cheat bread, which is also simply of wheat only, you shall, after your meal is dressed and bolted through a more coarse bolter than was used for your manchets, and put also into a clean tub, trough, or kimnel, take a sour leaven, that is a piece of such like leaven saved from a former batch, and well filled with salt, and so laid up to sour, and this sour leaven you shall break in small pieces into warm water, and then strain it; which done, make a deep hollow hole, as was before said, in the midst of your flour, and therein pour your strained liquor; then with your hand mix some part of the flour therewith, till the liquor be as thick as pancake batter, then cover it all over with meal, and so let it lie all that night; the next morning stir it, and all the rest of the meal well together, and with a little more warm water, barm, and salt to season it with, bring it to a perfect leaven, stiff, and firm; then knead it, break it, and tread it, as was before said in the manchets, and so mould it up in reasonable big loaves, and then bake it with an indifferent good heat: and thus according to these two examples before showed, you may bake any bread leavened or unleavened whatsoever, whether it be simple corn, as wheat or rye of itself, or compound grain as wheat and rye, or wheat, rye, and barley, or rye and barley, or any other mixed white corn; only, because rye is a little stronger grain than wheat, it shall be good for you to put to your water a little hotter than you did to your wheat.

Baking of brown bread.

For your brown bread, or bread for your hind servants, which is the coarsest bread for man's use, you shall take of barley two bushels, of pease two pecks, of wheat or rye a peck, a peck of malt; these you shall grind all together and dress it through a meal sieve, then putting it into a sour trough set liquor on the fire, and when it boils let one put on the water, and another with a mash-rudder stir some of the flour with it after it hath been seasoned with salt, and so let it be till the next day, and then, putting to the rest of the flour, work it up into a stiff leaven, then mould it and bake it into great loaves with a very strong heat: now if your trough be not sour enough to sour your leaven, then you shall either let it lie longer in the trough, or else take the help of a sour leaven with your boiling water: for you must understand, that the hotter your liquor is, the less will the smell or rankness of the pease be received. And thus much for the baking of any kind of bread, which our English housewife shall have occasion to use for the maintenance of her family.

General observations in the brew-house and bake-house.

As for the general observations to be respected in the brew-house or bake-house, they be these: first, that your brew-house be seated in so convenient a part of the house, that the smoke may not annoy your other more private rooms; then that your furnace be made close and hollow for saving fuel, and with a vent for the passage of smoke lest it taint your liquor; then that you prefer a copper before a lead, next that your mash vat be ever nearest to your lead, your cooler nearest your mash vat, and your gyle vat under your cooler, and adjoining to them all several clean tubs to receive your worts and liquors: then in your bake-house you shall have a fair bolting house with large pipes to bolt meal in, fair troughs to lay leaven in, and sweet safes to receive your bran: you shall have bolters, searces, ranges, and meal sieves of all sorts both fine and coarse; you shall have fair tables to mould on, large ovens to bake in, the soles thereof rather of one or two entire stones than of many bricks, and the mouth made narrow, square, and easy to be close covered: as for your peels, coal-rakes, malkins, and such like, though they be necessary yet they are of such general use they need no further relation. And thus much for a full satisfaction to all husbands and housewives of this kingdom touching brewing, baking, and all what else appertaineth to either of their offices.

FINIS

Glossary

abroach: open for use
achannes: acorns
alicant: dark, sweet, red wine, said to have been made in Spain
anacks: oatcake
Angulle wines: wine from the Angoulême region of France, near Bordeaux
apples of love: tomatoes
aqua composit: compound water

bag: stomach (of an animal)
barbel: large freshwater fish, related to carp
barberries: edible berry
barm: yeast
barstard: sweet wine
beetle: small wooden mallet
benjamin: resin from Oriental Sweetgum tree
betony: herb from the mint family
bleets: wild spinach
blink (in brewing): to make slightly more astringent
bolt: to sift
bolter: a sieve
brake: an instrument used for breaking or crushing
brawn: flesh or muscle

bray: to beat or crush to powder
broach: to pierce
bugloss: name for several plants in borage family with leaves resembling an ox's tongue
bullace: a wild plum
burnet: also known as bloodwort, but applied to several other plants
butt: a barrel

calamus aromaticus: aromatic reed
Candy cuit: sweet dessert wine from Crete, formerly known as Candia
capon: castrated fowl
caprik: sweet white wine
caraway: meridian fennel or Persian cumin
carbonadoes: meat boiled or grilled upon coals
centaury: plant believed in the past to have medicinal qualities
chawdron: sauce made from entrails and spices
chewet: pie made with minced meat
chibol: mild onion
chine: joint of meat
cob-iron: one of the irons on a turning spit
codling: an unripe apple
coffin: crust of a pie
collops: slices of meat (usually bacon)
conduit water: running water
corn-flag: species of gladiolus
crabs: crab apples
cuit: new wine boiled down and sweetened

doucet: spiced custard pie

dram: one-sixteenth of an ounce, or approximately 1.8 grams

draw: take from the oven or the spit

dredge: powder

dyer's grain: the dried bodies of the coccus insect, once thought to be a berry, used to make red dye

eager: sour or vinegary

earning: rennet

elecampane: horse-heal, a perennial composite used medicinally

eryngo: common name is sea-holly

farce: to stuff or season meat

farmes: cleaned intestines for making sausages

feaberry: gooseberry

fine: to clarify or refine

firkin: small cask

fistula: ulcer

flammery or flummery: food made from grain boiled into jelly

florentine: general term for a pie made in a pastry lined dish

flower-gentle: floramour

galantine: sauce made from blood

galingale: a plant with pungently aromatic roots, frequently used as a substitute for ginger

Gallaway wines: wine from Gaillac, in Southern France, known for its sparkling wines

gallipot: small earthenware pot used for ointments or medicines

germander: a plant from *Teucrium* species

gigot: leg or haunch

gillyflower: a clove-scented flower often used in salads

goldsmith's stone: touchstone, used by goldsmiths to test quality of gold

goodinyake: sweetmeat made from quinces

gravel: bladder stones

grits: coarse hulled grains

gum dragon: Tragacanth gum (dried sap of some Middle Eastern legumes)

gurnet: the gurnard

gyle: fermented wort for making vinegar or malt liquor

hartshorn: the horn or antler of a hart or wild deer

haslets: giblets

hind: a lesser servant or farm labourer

hogshead: a small barrel containing 40 to 60 gallons

horehound: herb and flowering plant

horseshoe: a flowering plant

hippocras: type of spiced wine strained through a conical cloth (hippocras bag)

hyssop: aromatic herb

ireos: orris, an aromatic powder made from the root of the white, Florentine iris

isinglass: fish gelatine

janacks: oatcakes

kimnel: a tub used in preparing bread, salt, meat, brewing and making cheese
knops: buds or seed vessels of flower
knots: knops or buds

labdanum: aromatic gum
lag: lack
langdebeef: ox tongue
lark-heel: larkspur
latten: an alloy similar to brass
lead: a cauldron or large kettle
limail: filings of metal
limbeck: upper part of a still where vapour condenses
ling: a saltwater fish, frequently salted and used in Lent
links: sausages
list: flank of pork
litharge: scum or foam of silver when the metal is refined
long: heavy or viscous

malkin: rag mop used to clean oven
malmsey: sweet fruity dessert wine
manchet: loaf of white bread
mange: food
marchpane: marzipan
mashing strom: (in brewing) an oblong wicker basket acting as a filter
mash-rudder: a paddle, most often used for mixing malt and water in brewing
mere sauce: marinade

metheglin: strong sweet drink made of honey and water and aromatic herbs

mithridate: medical compound; antidote to poison

morphew: disease that causes skin to scale

mugget: woodruff, wild baby's breath; (in cookery) intestines of calf or sheep

murrey: purple-red

muscadine: fruity sweet wine

neat: cow, cattle

nep: catmint

oak of Jerusalem: aromatic herb

olive: stew of meat cooked until meat disintegrates

orach: a tall annual herb, known as garden orach or mountain spinach

osey: sweet wine whine

panperdy: dish resembling modern-day French toast

pap: pulp

parel: ingredients used in clarifying wine; to give a 'parel' to wine

pearl: an opacity or cataract in the eye

peck: variable measure equivalent to approximately 9 litres

peel: baker's shovel, for removing bread from an oven

pellitory: lichwort, a plant of the nettle family

pennyroyal: a variety of mint

pepper, long: a variety of pepper (not now in general use)

pettitoes: trotters

pin and web: types of cataracts or opacities in the eye
pipe: barrel
pipkin: small earthenware pot or pan
pippin: cooking apple
pomecitron: citron
pottage: soup
pottle: measure equivalent to just over 2 litres
prick: become too acidic
print: (of pastry) press or mould into designs or shapes
Probatum est: 'It is proven'
purslane: more commonly known as a weed today but can be eaten
purtenance: animal's liver and lungs

quelquechose: meaning a 'something', a dish made up of a mixture of many things
quenebit: a spice-flavoured berry

Rhenish wines: wines from the region of the Rhine
ribwort: a narrow-leaved plantain
roche alum: rock alum
rochet: red gurnard
rosa solis: sundew
rout: order or a troop

sack: a sherry-type wine
sal gemma: rock salt
sallat: salad
sanders: sandalwood, with red, white and yellow varieties
sarcenet: soft silk-like material

saxifrage: the name (from Latin) means 'rock breaking', and was given to various plants which grew in the clefts of rocks

scotch: to score, cut deeply

scruple: measure equivalent to 20 grains, about a gram

scutcheons: shields and coats of arms

seam: clarified animal fat

searce: sift; a sieve

seethe: come to a boil; soak in liquid

Seres: (Jerez) town in Spain from which sherry takes its name

sester: a small measure of wine containing three or four gallons

shive: a slice

short: non-viscous (of wines)

short as moss: moss = mousse; stiff or frothy as mousse

short as snow: snow = whipped egg whites; stiff or frothy egg whites

shoveller: spoonbill (seabird with scoop-like beak)

sippet: a small slice of toasted or fried bread used to mop up gravy, soup or broth

skirret: plant with sweet, edible roots

smallage: also called wild celery or water parsley

smored: simmered or braised in a closed vessel

sodden: boiled

souse: to pickle

spike: French lavender

spikenard: sarsaparilla, trailing grape vine

splatted: split open

squinancy: quinsy (throat infection)

stillatory: a still
stint: a sandpiper
stock-dove: wild dove
stop: stuff (of poultry, etc.)
storax: aromatic gum
succory: a salad herb, closely related to the endive
sucket: a piece of fruit candied or preserved in sugar
sward: rind of bacon
swinge: to beat soundly or to whip

tansy: aromatic herb also known as mugwort; omelette or pudding flavoured with its juice
teal: small freshwater duck
tench: freshwater fish similar to carp
terms: menstrual period
trencher: a platter
tun: a barrel, the action of storing in a barrel
turnsole: a plant used to make a violet or deep-red dye
Tyre: sweet wine

veil: (of eggs) membrane
verjuice: juice of sour crab apples
vervain: verbena
vetches: the fruit of a leguminous plant

wallowish: insipid or tasteless
walm: spell of boiling
warden: a cooking widgeon: wild duck
washbrew: a dish similar to porridge
wort: the liquor made by an infusion of malt in water, from which beer and ale are fermented

GREAT  FOOD

THE CAMPAIGN FOR DOMESTIC HAPPINESS
Isabella Beeton

FIRMLY OF THE BELIEF THAT A HOME should
be run as an efficient military campaign, Mrs Beeton,
the doyenne of English cookery, offers timeless tips
on selecting cuts of meat, throwing a grand party
and hosting a dinner, as well as giving suggestions
on staff wages and the cost of each recipe.

With such delicious English classics as rabbit pie,
carrot soup, baked apple custard, and fresh lemonade
– as well as invalid's jelly for those days when stewed
eels may be a little too much – this is a wonderful
collection of food writing from the matriarch
of modern housekeeping.

'*Sublime . . . A Victorian gem*'
JULIAN BARNES

GREAT  FOOD

THROUGHOUT the history of civilization, food has been livelihood, status symbol, entertainment – and passion. The twenty fine food writers here, reflecting on different cuisines from across the centuries and around the globe, have influenced each other and continue to influence us today, opening the door to the wonders of every kitchen.